LYNTON & LYNMOUTH

The Golden Years

BRIAN PEARCE

EXMOOR BOOKS

First published in Great Britain in 2003

British Library Cataloguing-in-Publication Data
A CIP record for this title is available from the British Library

ISBN 0 86183 402 X

EXMOOR BOOKS
Official publisher to Exmoor National Park Authority
*Exmoor Books is a partnership between
Exmoor National Park Authority and Halsgrove*

Halsgrove House
Lower Moor Way
Tiverton, Devon EX16 6SS
T: 01884 243242
F: 01884 243325

sales@halsgrove.com
www.halsgrove.com

Printed and bound by Bookcraft, Midsomer Norton

❧ CONTENTS ❧

DEDICATION

*To Edward and Jane Nightingale in memory of
their father. Without their assistance this book
would not have been published.*

❧ INTRODUCTION ❧

This is one of a series of publications that invoke the early memories of people of my own age. It is a history book but it is difficult to envisage one's own lifetime as part of history. Lynton and Lynmouth retain the magnificent setting that earned the area the nickname 'the Switzerland of England' and, as a result, many feel that they have little altered. To today's children, however, the world of the 1950s and '60s will seem a very different one. However the place may or may not have altered, the way of life has certainly changed since most of these pictures were taken.

Some may say that the heyday of Lynton and Lynmouth was at the end of the nineteenth century. Certainly that was the boom time in terms of development – mostly linked with the tourist industry. Much of the boom was based on the optimism brought about by the coming of the railway, steamers and new roads that were to bring in hordes of wealthy tourists. Although much was built, that optimism was short-lived and, when the proposed pier did not materialise, the boom partly turned to bust. The First World War then changed the pattern of tourism and the wealthier tourists and second-home owners never returned. That boom era has been well recorded elsewhere and this new book concentrates on another, more recent, golden era for the parish.

The book covers the period from the end of the Second World War, when many were looking forward to a 'better Britain', through the 'never had it so good' years of the fifties and the 'swinging sixties' up to the slump of the 1980s which closed many local businesses. In the early part of this period film was not widely available. Family photographs are scarce and pictures of events and activities even more so. The book was prompted by the kind offer of Jane and Edward Nightingale to allow publication of the collection of their father, the late Dr Manners Nightingale, local GP through the time of the flood disaster. Edward has for some years used the collection as the basis for talks that he has given on the flood disaster. However, the collection contains many pictures from before and after that time and of many subjects depicting the life and personalities of the area; many will be new to local people.

I am also indebted to the Lee Abbey Fellowship, and particularly to John Law, for loan of photographs from their archive. Few people at Lee Abbey stay for more than a year or two but several have left behind a photographic record of their time within its community. I cannot thank them personally as all have moved on but it is clear from their photographs that all enjoyed their time there, and I am grateful to the Lee Abbey Fellowship for what they do. Their stories are largely visual but I am lucky to have a history of the Fellowship written by Richard More to place some of the pictures in context.

Another source of photographs has been the collection of the North Devon Athenaeum in Barnstaple. I was drawn to this collection by another publication in this series: *North Devon, the Golden Years* by Peter Christie. Although Peter had used some of the collection's pictures of Lynton and Lynmouth in his book, it was clear that there were several more to be revealed. The pictures are old press photographs taken on glass negatives for the *North Devon Journal Herald*. Some were used in the newspaper but others were never published. I am grateful to Les Franklin of the Athenaeum staff for sorting them and to the North Devon Record Office for their newspaper archive from which I could learn the background to some of the pictures.

Other pictures came from John Pedder. John took many pictures in the 1960s and '70s before his work as a local councillor took up much of his time. Many were used in local guidebooks and publicity brochures. His extensive knowledge of local people and events also proved invaluable. Another local 'oracle' is Bill Pryor, who has a collection of photographs which would bring the *Golden Years* up to date, and is a mine of information, particularly on railways and cinema. I also drew on Exmoor National Park Authority's collection within the Exmoor Photographic Archive based at Dulverton. Pictures credited to the Authority are copyright of various photographers. I am grateful, too, for the assistance of Margaret Pickford for sharing some of her holiday memories with me and loaning some of her snaps from her stays at 'The Hoe'.

CHAPTER ONE
❧ THE PLACE ❧

View over the Manor Green to the Foreland from the top of the cliff railway in 1952. This shows the beautiful setting which has been the main attraction of Lynton and Lynmouth for the last two centuries. At this time a debate was raging as to whether Exmoor should become a National Park; though it was mostly about money rather than scenery, the justification for National Park status stated: 'Lynton and Lynmouth have long been popular for quiet seaside holidays; Watersmeet, in the Lyn Valley, the Valley of Rocks and the cliffs and woods along this part of the coast, are unrivalled in the west of England.'

The Foreland from Station Hill, 1956. Since then many new houses have been built along Station Hill, some of them controversial in their skyline setting and in their context in a National Park. The view from them, however, is still as magnificent as in this picture. The only slight change has been the addition of a communications mast next to the old coastguard hut at Butter Hill on the Foreland.

-7-

Lynton from Summerhouse Hill in 1952. Looking back to the previous picture one can see the zigzag path from which this picture was taken. It is still a good viewpoint from which to look over Lynton. The view has changed somewhat with the burning down of the Royal Castle Hotel, and as the woodlands along the West Lyn are expanding.

Lynmouth harbour in 1939. This scene is still easily recognisable today yet the harbour wall, pier and tower have all been replaced. Protruding from the harbour wall is Turbal Rock, which was covered during the rebuilding and extension of the wall after the flood disaster. During the flood it had deflected the river and saved from destruction the buildings beyond it along Riverside Road.

Dr M Nightingale

Lynmouth harbour in 1949; another view that is also easily recognisable although much has changed. It is clear that there was still an active fishing industry at the time. Most of these vessels were amongst the first casualties of the flood. Owners watched helplessly as 19 boats were washed out to sea and sank or were smashed to pieces. Ken Oxenham lost three boats, including a trawler worth £2000, more than many houses cost in those days. All he managed to salvage was a brass bell inscribed with the trawler's name, Grateful. Ken's son, Matthew, now runs boat trips from the harbour.

Exmoor National Park Authority

Mars Hill c.1960. Until the mid-nineteenth century Mars Hill was the only built-up part of Lynmouth below Lyndale Bridge. The only way of reaching it was down the zigzag path from Lynton, lined with cottages, stores and smoke-houses for fishermen, now mostly accommodation for the Rising Sun Inn. Even at its height in the eighteenth century, the fishing industry, was mostly part-time, relying mainly on migratory fish which each had a short season. By the end of the eighteenth century the herrings, which at times brought prosperity but were always unreliable, had disappeared in any great quantity. Tourism took over and Lynmouth developed along the river below the hill.

Dr M Nightingale

Mars Hill through the arch of the Rhenish Tower in 1939. The tower was built around 1830 as a water tower holding sea water for the baths at the Bath Hotel. About twenty years later the battlemented top and fire basket were added for aesthetic reasons. It is not clear how its name came about as it was originally modelled on a picture of a tower on the coast of Lebanon, but it was suggested that it looked like a tower on the Rhine. It became a well-known landmark and when it was destroyed by the 1952 flood it was inevitable that it should be replaced.

Dr M Nightingale

The River Lyn at Lynmouth in 1948. Until the early-nineteenth century this was all part of the river mouth and delta; the river was not confined, and splayed out in finger-like channels over the delta. As the river is tidal here, high banks were built on each side to protect new buildings from flooding by the sea. The main channel, which had originally pressed up against the cliff below Lynton, was now moved eastwards to make way for Lynmouth Street, with houses on each side. The cottages and stores on the left were demolished to widen the river after the flood (some locals had always said that the river would one day return to its original course). After the flood the river was moved even farther from that course, and Riverside Road now runs where the river did in this picture.

From a local postcard

A view down Lynmouth Street in the 1940s. This is now Riverside Road. The view shows a block of buildings that was demolished after the flood to allow for the widening of the West Lyn river. To the left is the Granville House Hotel, with the West Lyn Café, middle, and the Lyn Valley Hotel, right. The latter was for many years in the hands of the Bevan family, who also owned the Lyndale Hotel at the time of the flood. The Bevans provided guests with deep-sea fishing and walks in the Glen Lyn grounds.

'The Little Blue and White Shop' was one of Pedder's shops in Lynmouth Street, pictured here in the early 1960s. Before the war it was a hairdresser's and afterwards it became a gift shop, then was demolished about 1966 and rebuilt as 'Cartwheels' with an apartment above. The Pedder family has been in Lynton and Lynmouth for generations, owning several shops. During the First World War they traded as the Crown Trading Company, with grocery, drapery and butchers' stores in Lynton and Lynmouth, a Post Office, corn and coal merchants and carriage proprietors. In 1954 a proposal to open shops on Sundays for holidaymakers was turned down on religious grounds.

John Pedder

Comic postcards on display in Lynmouth in September 1954. Although very popular, such cards were still seen as crude by many. In 1956 nearly 2000 'obscene' and 'suggestive' postcards were seized by police in Ilfracombe and destroyed.

Dr M Nightingale

Lyndale Cross c.1951. This is another scene that was changed forever by the flood. The only building now remaining is Shelley's Cottage Hotel – the white building in the background. The buildings to the right of the picture – a fruit shop and Gospel Chapel – were swept away. The Lyndale Hotel, seen on the left, was later demolished to make way for a car park; outside stands PC Derek Harper, who was awarded the George Medal for his rescue services during the disaster.

Dr M. Nightingale

Combined efforts to publicise Lynton and Lynmouth as a tourist destination started with the Hoteliers' Association in 1938. Meetings were held in an hotel and there was no Tourist Information Centre; this came with the setting up of the Lynton & Lynmouth Publicity Association during the 1950s. Originally based at the bus station off Lee Road, following its closure the Centre moved to its present site at the Town Hall in 1985. The National Park Authority set up an information stall at the Lyn and Exmoor Museum in the 1960s, and its own centre in the old Parish Rooms on Watersmeet Road in 1975, when this picture was taken. Its role was educational rather than being seen as in competition with the Tourist Information Centre. Latterly, it was run by Peggy Parry from Barbrook. It relocated to the Pavilion in 1982 and in the first full year the number of customers rose from an average 10,000 per year to 120,000. In 1990 they topped 200,000.

Exmoor National Park Authority

The Anglican church of St John the Baptist at Lynmouth was opened in 1870 as an offshoot of the parish church of the same name at Countisbury. It survived the flood disaster intact and a vestry was added after the flood, with a donation from the US Airforce. Inside is a list of the 27 people who died in the disaster and a memorial to John Ward, last coxswain of the Lynmouth lifeboat. The Parish Hall alongside was originally an art gallery but was given to the people of the town during the First World War.

North Devon Athenaeum

John Pedder

A view up the East Lyn in the 1940s, with Tors Road on the left and the power station on the right, with its workers' cottages above. Lynton and Lynmouth were among the first settlements in Britain to have electric light, supplied by a hydro-electric power station that was built alongside the East Lyn in 1890. The water came from higher up the river via a leat and pipe, the power reaching locals via underground cables. With increasing demand, a pumped storage scheme, possibly the first in the world, was installed to use off-peak electricity to pump water to a tank on Summerhouse Hill. The water was released again to power new turbines at peak times. New and more efficient turbines were gradually added and, when demand outstripped production, supplementary diesel generators were installed. In 1952 when the flood struck, South Western Electricity Board, who owned the power station, were already working to bring mains electricity to the area from a new power station at Yelland. The leat to the Lynmouth station was quickly washed out and it continued as long as possible on diesel power before being flooded. Afterwards the mains was connected to the existing underground cables so that there was no need to rebuild the station.

Dr M Nightingale

Longpool in the East Lyn above Watersmeet in 1957. This calm scene shows no signs of the flood of five years earlier.

From a local postcard

North Devon Athenaeum

The Hoe was built as the home of Sir Thomas Hewitt, one of the town's great benefactors. The story goes that he visited Lynton on honeymoon and asked his wife if she would like to live there. When she agreed he gave her a stone and asked her to throw it and where it landed he would build her a house. Although it ended up on what could be described as a cliff, he had the foundations dynamited out and an imposing house built. The extensive grounds included Hollerday Hill and the Valley of Rocks. Visitors were able to use the zigzag paths through his gardens to walk between Lynton and Lynmouth, although in later life he was more keen to have privacy. After he died in 1923 the house became an hotel. Regular guests in the 1960s, '70s and '80s, during which time the hotel changed hands several times, were Margaret Pickford and her family. Margaret's daughter was an avid Enid Blyton fan and thought that there must be secret passages behind all of the wood panelling. The views along the coast and flashes from the lighthouse made her think that there were smugglers. More recently, it changed its name to Hewitt's and for a while was a restaurant.

The well-known Lynton & Lynmouth Cliff Railway in the 1950s. It had run smoothly and carried millions of passengers since it was built in 1890, at which time it was the steepest railway in Britain. It survived the flood disaster unscathed but in 1960 one of its cars was derailed. Passengers were shaken but not hurt. It was the only accident in the railway's history, apart from the time when a dog's tail was run over.

Exmoor National Park Authority

St Vincent's Cottage, here pictured in the 1970s, is one of the oldest houses in Lynton, with a stone slab roof. In the early 1960s Lynton Urban District Council owned it, and John Pedder and Harry Sutton, local members of the Exmoor Society saved it from demolition. They saw it as a suitable place for an Exmoor museum and the Council let the Society use it on a peppercorn rent. It was opened in July 1962, with downstairs rooms focussing on the social history of Exmoor, and upstairs rooms dedicated to Lynton and Lynmouth.

Sinai Hill is one of Lynton's oldest and steepest streets. It led to Mount Sinai, a popular viewpoint for Victorian visitors. In 1869 a water tank was built on the hill to replace Lynton's old springwater supply. When the railway came in 1898, porters had to push luggage barrows up and down this very steep road, which was little more than a muddy footpath, known as Shamble Way, at its top end. Passengers had to go back towards Barbrook and down to the top of Lynmouth Hill to access Lynton by road. The road at Station Hill was not built until 1927. The top of the road has been tarmacked relatively recently but a sign declares it unfit for motors.

A view down Lydiate Lane in the 1950s. Before Lee Road became the main thoroughfare in the late nineteenth century, this was Lynton's main road, leading to and from Barnstaple, along which the settlement had expanded. It then continued westwards straight over the down to Dean.

North Devon Athenaeum

After the Second World War there was a great housing shortage nationally. During the war Lynton Urban District Council were already thinking about a post-war housing scheme. They decided to buy a field at Keals Croft, adjacent to Lydiate Lane, for council houses. They were designed by the Council's own surveyor, Fred Gibbs. Work started as soon as war finished in 1945.

The top of Queen Street in the early 1980s. John Pedder took this picture, as he owned the shops on either side of the street. The street was originally Lynton's main street and called Pig Hill. It had a stream running down it, which was the town's water supply. The street was renamed after Queen Victoria's Diamond Jubilee.

John Pedder

A rooftop view of Lee Road in the 1940s. In the centre is the Methodist Church with the Town Hall to its right. The Town Hall was built in 1900 and paid for by Sir George Newnes, who lived on Hollerday Hill behind. The Methodist Church was built ten years later, replacing an earlier building. In 1939 there were moves to curb the opening hours of the Town Hall for fear of IRA bombing.

A view from the Rectory, next to the Methodist Church, across Lee Road in the 1940s. On the left is Elliott's Garage and just out of the picture on the right was the Lynton Cottage Hospital, which had been there since 1874. In the middle is the chemist's shop that still exists. To the left of it was a cake shop and, to the right, a haberdasher's. There were other chemists on Church Hill and at Lynmouth.

Bill Pryor

Nature takes over the ruins of Hollerday House in the early 1950s. The house was built for publishing magnate Sir George Newnes in 1893. Hollerday Hill at the time was treeless and open fields but Sir George laid out gardens and planted many trees so that now it is well wooded. The house was burnt down in 1913, after his death, and was finally demolished in 1956 as an exercise by Royal Marine Commandos. Local children had been making camps in it and the ruins were not safe. Some of the stones were used in the rebuilding of flood-damaged bridges and other structures.

Dr M Nightingale

This picture is of the Valley of Rocks end of Lee Road in 1939. To the right of the picture can be seen the relatively new and empty cemetery. The previous cemetery, on the side of Hollerday Hill, where Sir George Newnes was buried, had become full.

Dr M Nightingale

This picture is taken from further into the Valley of Rocks c.1950. The fields to the right were soon to become a static caravan site that for some years was to disfigure the beauty of the valley. In 1968 the Devon National Park Committee purchased the site in order to remove it and replace it with a picnic area.

A coach unloads passengers at the roundabout in the Valley of Rocks in the 1950s. It was near the roundabout that prehistoric stone circles and field boundaries were rediscovered after extensive fires in 1956. There had been a much larger stone circle near that point but that was destroyed in the mid-nineteenth century. As more and more visitors came by car, service buses stopped running to the valley, although there was an attempt with the 'Coastlink' scheme, introduced in 1976, to link bus services with walks along the South West Coast Path.

Exmoor National Park Authority

According to *Cooper's Guidebook* of 1853 there had been many goats in the Valley of Rocks but numbers were reduced because they butted sheep over the cliffs. This story was picked up by RD Blackmore and in *Lorna Doone* there was a scene where a black goat butted a sheep from Castle Rock. Towards the end of the nineteenth century they were removed altogether. The white Saanen goats in the Valley of Rocks are thought to have been introduced from the royal herd at Sandringham in 1897. Guidebooks of the 1920s suggest that there were only a dozen or so. By the time these photographs were taken they had become more numerous and more of a nuisance. One billy in particular was so used to wandering down Lee Road and raiding gardens that one day the doors of a Council meeting were flung open and the goat thrown inside, by way of protest.

Goats on Castle Rock, 1952.

Saanen goats in the Valley of Rocks in 1951.

Saanen billy goat 1951.

The goats in these pictures died off in the hard winter of 1962/63 but were soon replaced by similar goats – some say through dumping of unwanted goats there. Old British goats were introduced in 1976 in order to introduce new blood. From 1984 the Saanen bloodline was gradually taken out by culling to help preserve the Old British variety, which is the closest breed to wild goats in Britain. A Friends of the Goats group was set up in 1997 to manage the goats and find homes for the offspring.

CHAPTER TWO
❧ THE PEOPLE ❧

Dr Manners Nightingale, local GP and keen amateur photographer, took many of the photographs in this book. As a doctor he knew most people in Lynton and Lynmouth, and local characters were amongst his favourite photographic subjects.

Edward Nightingale

Edward Nightingale

Manners Nightingale in 1947. He was forty-four at the time of the flood. A very modest man, he worked tirelessly through the disaster to save as many people as he could. After driving into Lynmouth, he and his brother Neville helped to evacuate a large number of people trapped in the Lyn Valley Hotel. The brothers then scrambled down the cliff face behind the Bath Hotel. They managed to climb on to the roof of a shop and get a rope across the street to evacuate many more visitors from the Bath Hotel. Dr Nightingale then tied a rope around himself and went off to help others, wading through the torrent running down the street. He kept working through the height of the flood from 9.00pm until 3.30am. The family took in some of those made homeless.

Dr Manners Nightingale holding his Leica camera, photographed by his son, Edward, in 1950. Manners was born and brought up in South Africa but qualified as a doctor at St Thomas's in London. Straight afterwards, in 1938, he arrived at Lynton to take up a practice, living next to his surgery at Garson House. At the time there were two practices in Lynton but he joined forces with Dr Hotson under the new National Health scheme in 1947. He retired in 1969 and died in 1974 after a long illness, contracted at the time of the flood disaster.

Dr M Nightingale

Young Edward Nightingale being escorted for a ride by Dorothea Nancekivell. This picture was taken on a popular circular ride out from the Tally Ho! stables in Cross Street. Here they stopped for a drink at Ye Olde Cottage Inne (now the Bridge Inn) at Lynbridge, where there was a mounting block outside the door.

Dr M Nightingale

A groom at the 'Tally Ho!' stables in Cross Street in 1940, possibly Fanny Duncan.

One can easily guess that Billy Harris, photographed in 1949, was a painter and decorator. He worked for one of the various Hobbs family building firms. He was also an odd-job man and helped the Nightingales with their garden, whilst his wife, Dorothy, helped them in the house.

Bob Jones outside his garage in the 1940s, where he serviced and repaired motorcycles. He was main agent for Lambretta scooters in the days of the 'Mods'. Bob was a keen driver as well as mechanic and drove regularly in the Easter hill-climb trials on Beggar's Roost. The Jones family is well known in Lynton. Bob's brother, Douglas, was known as a footballer. Their father, Witney, and grandfather, also Bob, were directors of the cliff railway company and grandfather Bob was the original engineer of the railway. Bob Jnr later also became its engineer.

Dr M Nightingale

Ray Elliott photographed in his workshop in 1942. Ray and Mark Elliott were partners in Elliott's Garage at the corner of Cross Street and Lee Road. They had inherited a coachbuilding business from their father, later turning it into a garage.

Bill Prideaux photographed in 1968. Bill was blacksmith at the smithy, which was at the back of a lane just off Church Hill. When it closed it became the Old Smithy Museum for a few years.

John Pedder

Charlie Litson at Lynmouth in 1948, member of a well-known Lynton family. Before the flood Charlie would stand at the entrance to the Glen Lyn Gorge in a white coat, issuing tickets for the walk up the gorge. His brother, Harry, was drowned in the flood.

Bill Durman, photographed in 1951, was a window cleaner. He was also CO in charge of the local St John Ambulance Brigade at the time of the flood, when the Brigade was much needed.

'Carver Doone' Ridd and pony in 1945. 'Carver' was a well-known local character. He became self-styled guardian of the goats in the Valley of Rocks.

Locals were renowned for their longevity. This is a picture of Granny Squire at Cheriton in 1950 when she was aged ninety-seven.

Charlie Priscott photographed in 1945. The Priscotts were farmers just outside Lynton.

Alfie Stiling photographed near his home, Barham Cottage near West Ilkerton, in 1940. He always walked into Lynton with his back-pack to fetch provisions and was a favourite subject for Manners Nightingale's camera. Alfie lived with Grace Wensley. When he died she left his body there for a week before calling for the doctor to take it away 'because the rats were gnawing at his toes'.

CHAPTER THREE
❧ ACTIVITIES ❧

Hunting was one of the attractions for early visitors to Lynton and Lynmouth. As early as 1808 the Valley of Rocks Hotel was advertising that hunting was available for its customers. In the mid-nineteenth century a pack of staghounds was kept at Lynbridge. Otter hounds often met at the Lyn Valley Hotel at Lynmouth. The Exmoor Foxhounds, nicknamed the 'Stars of the West', developed from a pack kept by Nicholas Snow at Oare between 1869 and 1889. This pack stayed at Oare until after the Second World War, when the kennels moved to Simonsbath. The regular meets are on Mondays, Wednesdays and Saturdays. It became a tradition for the foxhounds to meet outside the Town Hall soon after it was built in 1900, particularly on Boxing Day.

A meet outside the Town Hall in 1939. The two young riders are Jean and Ann Roberts. Lt-Col R Alexander was master from 1937 to 1940 and at the time of this photograph the huntsman was H Lang.

The Exmoor Foxhounds continued to meet during the war, although not as regularly, and after the war the Boxing Day meet was normally at Lynmouth. Lt-Col Guy Jackson was master from 1940 until his death in 1960. In the latter years he was joint master with Jack Hosegood. Guy had no legs but this did not prevent him from riding. This is him with the walking sticks in the centre of a picture of a Boxing Day meet in 1948. The crowds are watching from the Falls and Granville hotels across the road.

Dr M Nightingale

Another picture of the 1948 Boxing Day meet outside the Lyndale Hotel. Behind are the greengrocer's and the Glen Lyn Garage which were later swept away in the flood.

Dr M Nightingale

This undated picture shows Miss S Faulkner who was master from 1940 until 1946. On the right is Mr G Lock.

The first Boxing Day meet after the flood disaster in 1952. Local people were keen that life returned to normal after the flood. It was now impractical to meet outside the Lyndale Hotel, so they met outside the Rising Sun instead and meets continued there until the 1990s.

Girls riding along the Esplanade at the 1952 meet.

The hounds moving off along Lynmouth Street in 1952.

The field moving across the bottom of Lynmouth Hill, where there was a temporary car park in front of Shelley's Cottage Hotel.

A Boxing Day meet outside the Rising Sun in the early 1970s. Victor Martin was the huntsman on the grey horse. Jim Butcher, a well-known West Country reporter was standing above the wall in the middle. The landlady giving out drinks was Stella Vanner. Jack Hosegood was master or joint master, and sometimes huntsman as well, from 1960 until the 1980s. In recent years the meet has been at Blackmoor Gate because Lynmouth became too congested.

The Devon and Somerset Stag-hounds on the Manor Green in the 1960s. The staghounds do not meet at Lynmouth but were here giving a display for one of the annual Spring Festival events, which ran for several years in the '60s and '70s.

Maypole dancing on the Manor Green during a Spring Festival in 1968. The dancing display was organised by Muriel Pearcey, schoolmistress at Countisbury.

Morris dancing on the Esplanade during a rather soggy Spring Festival in 1968.

Riding was, and still is a popular pastime in the area. Before traffic became too heavy it was relatively easy to ride out from the centre of Lynton. In the 1940s there were two stables in Cross Street, one of which was the 'White Browband', run by Charlie Halsgrove whose brother was chairman of the local Council. This picture shows the Tally Ho! stables, which stood where the entrance to the fire station is now and was run by the Nancekivell family of Cloud Farm at Oare. In the centre is Dorothea Nancekivell, who later emigrated to Ireland.

Another view of the Tally Ho! stables. The rider is Mr Pennington who owned the Royal Castle Hotel.

North Devon Athenaeum

Holman Park has been the focus of many of Lynton's sporting activities. It was named after John Holman, a local benefactor who gave the town Hollerday Estate, which included the Valley of Rocks and Hollerday Hill. He bought the site and laid out the grounds before giving it to the Town Council in 1927. It is now home to the Lynton & Lynmouth Football Club. This picture from the early 1950s shows the tea hut at the ground. On the far right, in the football club's new post-war strip, is Douglas Jones. Next to him is Mr Hendry and far left is Bertie Popham, both keen supporters of the club.

Bill Pryor

A carnival ran from Holman Park in Lynton during the 1950s, '60s and '70s. It was difficult to link up with Lynmouth for this activity and the enthusiasm and the fashion for carnivals waned. This photograph from c.1955 shows the Ley family float with their spelling of the 'Reconstruction of Lynmouth'. Over the back of the lorry is a stone model of Lyndale Bridge, which was rebuilt during the winter of 1954/55. On the right is Michael Sharp of Lynmouth, the only person in the photograph still alive at the time of writing.

An entry in the 1956 carnival from the 'Children's Wonderland' shop in Lynton.

North Devon Athenaeum

A Motor Club entry into the carnival c.1970. Adge Cutler and the Wurzels had just visited Lynton Town Hall at the height of their fame and packed it with an audience of 700. The man in drag is Harry Sutton, founder of the Lyn and Exmoor Museum.

John Pedder

An early-1970s' entry, possibly from Lee Abbey. It seems to refer to traffic problems and calls for the reopening of the railway.

Lee Abbey Fellowship

North Devon Athenaeum

The bowling green is along Lee Road, near Holman Park. It is still well used from spring to autumn and the club plays away matches indoors in the winter. A green had been built in 1905 for the town by Sir George Newnes in his grounds on Hollerday Hill. In this picture the Lee Road green was relatively new. It shows the reopening of the Bowling Club after the Second World War. Second from left is Dorothy Slater, who became chairman of the Council at the time of the flood disaster. 'Jack' Pedder, fifth from left, was then chairman. The small man with glasses in the middle was Town Clerk Leonard Ridge.

In 1891 Sir George Newnes paid for Warren Field in the Valley of Rocks to be levelled for a cricket ground, and later for a thatched pavilion there. This was burnt down by young vandals in the 1990s and rebuilt with a slate roof. The cricket club, founded in 1876, played on different sites, including the Warren in the Valley of Rocks before Sir George Newnes donated that site. It was a surprisingly good pitch for such a rocky site, the two main problems being rabbits and the wind. In the 1950s it took several years to erect a rabbit-proof fence around the ground. The wild goats, however, learned to jump over the stiles. It can also be difficult to keep the bails on the stumps because of the wind. There were normally two matches a week in the summers of the 1950s. There are now two teams, each with a fixture a week from April to September.

A view of a cricket match in July 1956.

Rolling the pitch in July 1956. John Shires is the cricketer seen left and Bert Tuckey is on the right.

A view from above the pavilion in 1957.

Boys keep the score in 1950.

Dr M Nightingale

Eric Edmunds, a keen cricketer and friend of the Nightingale family in 1950. It looks as if he had a good season in 1950 from the score on the back of the photo.

Raising funds for the Cricket Club at their annual fête on the Manor Grounds in 1952. Club members are, from left to right: Geoff Burgess, who was an administrator for British Airways; John Shires, a local restaurateur; Tom Parish, who worked in Lloyd's Bank; Nim Rumbelow, who had a grocer's shop on Lee Road; and Cliff Compton, who ran the chemist's in Lynmouth that was washed away shortly after this picture was taken.

North Devon Athenaeum

North Devon Athenaeum

The Town Hall has for many years been home to productions of the Dramatic Society and Lyn Minstrels. This picture shows a production of Sacred Flame *in 1953.*

The Lyn Minstrels traditionally put on shows during Lent so that they can practise through the winter and be finished before the summer tourist season starts; many locals are too busy in summer months to join in such activities. A few of the scenes would be practised as a Christmas entertainment for senior citizens. This picture is from a show performed in the 1960s.

John Pedder

A Parisian scene from a Lyn Minstrels show in the 1960s.

The Town Hall cinema in the 1980s. Major Blackhurst had had several cinemas, known as 'BB' cinemas, throughout the West Country and towards the end of his life had kept one on Sinai Hill at Lynton. Following his death in 1961, a cinema was set up in the Town Hall and films were shown in summer, run by Bill Pryor throughout the 1980s. Recently a new cinema opened in the former Methodist Chapel next to the Town Hall. Much of the interior of the 'BB' cinema remains intact.

North Devon Athenaeum

The annual free Christmas children's party at the Town Hall in 1956, the event's 25th anniversary. This was swelled by evacuees during the war. Then it took place at the Pavilion, where they were given a show with magic and puppet acts.

Dr M Nightingale

Every community had its Civil Defence volunteers who were taught how to cope in the event of a nuclear war. Here at Bottom Meadow car park in 1954 an instructor has arrived to show the local group how to construct a field kitchen from bricks and dustbins.

A group calling themselves Dickensian Carols dressed up in Victorian costume every Christmas from 1961 to 1986. They serenaded locals to raise money for charity, mostly for Dr Barnardo's. Jim Saunders, well-known singer of local folk songs and carols, is amongst this group, seen outside the Rising Sun at Lynmouth in the late 1960s.

Dickensian Carols on Church Hill at Lynton in the late 1960s.

Dr M Nightingale

A tidal bathing pool had been built on the West Beach at Lynmouth in Victorian times, serving a useful purpose for swimmers at low tide. In the late 1920s and early 30s it was improved with concrete walls and the posts for the diving boards were replaced with steel rails from the cliff railway. In 1945 the bathing pool, seen here in 1951, needed repairs but these were postponed by plans for a new pool on Manor Beach. The pool was, however, still well used in the 1960s.

Margaret Pickford

Sheila Pickford and her cousin Julie on the Manor Green putting green in 1968. The Pickfords were regular visitors to Lynton, staying at The Hoe.

Bell-ringers at St Mary's church in the 1950s. From left to right: Beatrice Souttar (née Bowden), Eileen Dyson, Freddy Baker (the local postman), Elizabeth Wage and Barbara Martin.

A bring-and-buy stall at the church fête in 1951.

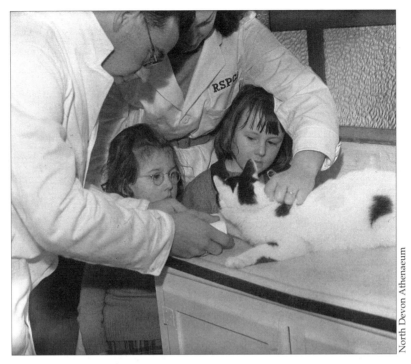

North Devon Athenaeum

Children at the Lynton RSPCA Centre in 1954. The centre, accessed from Hume Avenue, was a small outbuilding in the garden of Mrs Whitney-Jones, who lived at Longmead.

Exmoor National Park Authority

Devon County Council employed a warden for their part of the National Park from 1963. Much of his time at first was spent providing information at Combe Martin. Somerset County Council became the National Park Authority in 1974, employing Alan Dudden as warden for the North Devon area in 1975. At that time Hollerday Hill was becoming rather neglected and overgrown and there were several attempts to involve children in its maintenance. Here, Alan is planting trees with Kevin Dyer, as part of a project with Ilfracombe School.

CHAPTER FOUR
❧ EVENTS ❧

Apart from the flood in 1952 there was little that happened in Lynton and Lynmouth during the 'Golden Years' that made national news. Times were, however, changing and much that was happening nationally affected the area.

Dr M Nightingale

Fireworks for VE Day. There was a week of celebrations for Victory in Europe in May 1945. Bells were rung and there were thanksgiving services in the churches. Children were given a free cinema show followed by tea, then sports at Holman Park. That evening there was a free dance for the adults at the Town Hall, attended by 800 people. The next day a concert was given for the two schools that had been evacuated to Lynton. The week was ended by a Thanksgiving parade. Similar events took place for VJ celebrations in August, although many of the evacuees had gone by then. Many bonfires were lit.

Exmoor National Park Authority

This 1930s' scene shows the towing of the Pritchard Frederick Gayner *along the Esplanade in the 1930s to launch at the West Beach, done for show on the annual Lifeboat Day. The* Pritchard Frederick Gayner, *was just a 'pulling' (rowing) boat and the motor boats at Ilfracombe and Minehead could cover the area, so Lynmouth lost its service in 1945. Eventually she was sold as a pleasure boat and finally sailed out of the harbour amid VE Day celebrations. The boathouse was destroyed in the 1952 flood disaster.*

North Devon Athenaeum

This picture from December 1948 shows a board outlining the history of the Lynmouth lifeboats. Either side are the two surviving lifeboatmen who took part in the famous 'overland launch' in 1899, when the Lynmouth lifeboat Louisa *was manhandled over the moors to be launched at Porlock Weir to rescue a ship being blown ashore in a gale. On the left is William Richards, who was born in 1862 and died in 1963. His fellow crew member, Captain George Richards, right, had always maintained that a time would come when the Lyn river would flood and revert to its original course along Lynmouth Street.*

North Devon Athenaeum

Here, the lifeboatmen are joined by others associated with Lynmouth's last lifeboat. Next to the board is Tom Bevan, local lifeboat secretary, later chairman of the Council and owner of the Lyndale Hotel at the time of the flood. On the far right is EJ 'Jack' Pedder, the chairman of the Council during much of the war. He was a signalman for Lynmouth's last lifeboat. His father, also EJ Pedder, was Lloyd's shipping agent at the time of the 'overland launch', who went out with the lifeboat crew from Porlock Weir

John Pedder

The Cardiff Queen *off Lynmouth in the 1960s. Steamers first started calling at Lynmouth in 1830. By 1894, 7000 passengers a year were landing there by steamer. Landing was not always possible, owing to rough seas, but long-running plans for a pier were shelved in 1901 amid accusations that it would encourage riff-raff to visit what was a 'genteel' resort. Immediately after the Second World War, Campbells built two new steamers, partly for routes out of Ilfracombe. The* Cardiff Queen *and* Bristol Queen *were finished in 1947. They made regular trips up and down the Bristol Channel in summer and often called at Lynmouth. However, diesel propeller steamers became more economical and the* Cardiff Queen *was taken out of service in 1966. The* Bristol Queen*, which was considered to be the ultimate in paddle steamer design, was given a major overhaul but was damaged a year later and not considered economical to repair.*

North Devon Athenaeum

The first passengers to arrive from a paddle steamer – the Cardiff Queen *– after the Second World War, in June 1949. Between the wars 'Jack' Pedder was local agent for the steamers, which had called frequently during the summer season. Motor boats used to tow 'packet boats' of passengers out to the steamers. By the time of this picture two launches, the Lynmouth Queen I and II, which had been used to offload supplies and passengers for Lundy, were being worked as passenger launches.*

Lynmouth greeted the passengers enthusiastically and the chairman of the Council, SC Willshire, gave a speech wishing for fine weather and plenty more days when the passengers could land. At high tide the passengers could embark or disembark on the beach below the Rock House. After the flood disaster the debris brought down by the flood was used during the reconstruction and in the process the beach was raised by 18 feet.

North Devon Athenaeum

The steamer launches were still well used until the mid-1960s, when this picture was taken. In recent years the Waverley, *the last working sea-going paddle steamer, has made calls at Lynmouth during summer seasons in the Bristol Channel.*

A flock of sheep being driven towards a camera in the process of making a film at the foot of Lynmouth Hill in 1946. In 1963 the area was put on the map when a version of Lorna Doone, *starring Bill Travers, was filmed locally.*

The opening of the school playground at Lynton c.1952. Mrs Blackhurst had campaigned for the playground for some years but it had conflicted with plans to turn Bottom Meadow into a car park. Her husband, Major Blackhurst, who ran the cinema on Sinai Hill, is seen second from the left. The chairman of the Council is Fred Halsgrove.

North Devon Athenaeum

John Pedder

Prince Philip took an hour out of a scheduled visit to North Devon to see the flood damage at Lynmouth in October 1952, accompanied by Earl Fortescue, the Lord Lieutenant of Devon, and Dorothy Slater, chairman of the Urban District Council. Here he is seen with Dorothy Slater and 'Jack' Pedder. Locals even managed to put out a welcome banner and buntings amongst the debris of the flood. The A39 had been cleared a month earlier and his motor cavalcade was able to descend Countisbury Hill and cross Lyndale Bridge. From Lynmouth he went up the cliff railway and visited some of the homeless at their caravan site in Holman Park. The first permanent home for those made homeless by the flood – a bungalow – had already been erected and the Prince declared that open. He said that he would return to see the reconstruction of Lynmouth, a trip which he eventually made in November 2002.

Before the flood Lynton Housing Committee had a list of 23 families waiting for homes. The flood then destroyed 37 homes and so there was urgent need for new housing. Red tape was waived so that the committee could start immediate construction of 30 houses on six sites off Lee Road. A decision was taken to build 28 Cornish Unit houses – prefabricated yet permanent houses, made of concrete panels, which could be erected quickly – at Longmead. Despite objections to spoiling the beautiful approach to the Valley of Rocks, eight houses went up in four weeks at Hume Avenue. The remaining 20 houses were finished by January 1953 and the site for a proposed new school was sacrificed in the process.

North Devon Athenaeum

As well as the Cornish Units, other quickly erected units known as Wilson-block houses were constructed. Two of these went up in two months and were donated to the local council by the builders, Costain of Plymouth. The owner of the company, Richard Costain, handed over the keys to the council during lunch at the Imperial Hotel in December 1952. In this picture he is seen shaking hands with the first tenant, Mrs Litson, whose husband was drowned in the flood. He is between councillors 'Jack' Pedder and Dorothy Slater. Mr Pedder wore many hats and in this context he was chairman of the Housing Committee. The houses, off Lee Road were named Costain Villas.

September 1952 and homeless Lynmouthians are being given a free coach trip to Ilfracombe by local councillors.

North Devon Athenaeum

After the flood Lynton and Lynmouth were visited by dignitaries from all over the country offering assistance. Several mayors offered housing in their own towns but it was decided that it would be better to keep families in their own communities. Many people helped by giving or loaning caravans and the Hotpoint company donated a fully equipped laundry for the caravan site. In this picture from October 1952 the Lord Mayor of Birmingham is seen with Sally Hobbs, one of the laundry supervisors who worked at Lynton's main laundry in Cavendish Place. The laundry was like a small factory with a tall, smoky chimney which caused many complaints. A launderette stands on the site today.

The funerals of the first 13 victims of the flood disaster took place in August 1952 at Lynton Cemetery. Six members of the Floyd family were buried together. Here, in October 1953, Tom Bevan lays a wreath on the grave of Maud and William Watts following a memorial service.

North Devon Athenaeum

In October 1953 the Bishop of Exeter dedicated a memorial vestry in St John's church, Lynmouth. The vestry had been paid for by members of the US Air Force serving in Britain. In it was placed a tablet listing all of those who died in the flood.

All over the country there were celebrations for the Queen's Coronation Day on 2 June 1953. As with previous coronations, it was common to give children commemorative mugs. The author received a Bible. Here children are being given their mugs by Lynton Urban District Council.

North Devon Athenaeum

The Coronation was accompanied by street parties and bonfires, this one destined to be the Lynton bonfire at Holman Park.

John Pedder

The wedding of Norman West, an airline pilot and rugby player, and Shirley Medway, a Sister at the Cottage Hospital, in 1963. They were taking part in a local tradition in which a garlanded rope was placed by bachelors to block the way of the bride and groom from the church. The latter had to pay for the rope to be cut by handing over or throwing coins to the onlookers but had to be careful not to empty his pockets in case of another barrier lying around the corner. The tradition was reserved mostly for those who could be expected to pay generously and was last practised at Lynmouth in the early 1980s.

A similar idea is employed for the opening of the Exmoor section of the then South West Peninsula Coast Path on the Foreland in July 1975. Speaking to local councillors in 1952, Lord Merthyr of the National Parks Commission outlined plans for the National Park and the Coast Path. Exmoor became a National Park two years later, with Lynton UDC being the only local council to give the idea support. The Coast Path took a bit longer! Here, on the right, Dr Gerardo Budowski, Director General of the IUCN (International Union for the Conservation of Nature and Natural Resources) opened the path by cutting the garland. In the centre stands Maj-Gen Dare Wilson, Exmoor's first National Park officer.

Exmoor National Park Authority

Exmoor National Park Authorty

Another long-distance path, the Two Moors Way, was opened a year later. It runs from Ivybridge, south of Dartmoor, to Lynmouth. At the opening ceremony on the Manor Green can be seen the Mayor, John Pedder.

North Devon Athenaeum

Here in May 1982 the Girl Maureen lands at the harbour slipway. She had been a Padstow fishing boat but originally was an old 'pulling' lifeboat similar to the Louisa which was used in the famous 'overland launch' of 1899. She was purchased by LOLA (the Lynmouth Old Lifeboat Association), restored to her original condition as a lifeboat and renamed Louisa II. Her arrival coincided with the opening of the new Exmoor National Park Visitor Centre in the Pavilion, where the lifeboat was to be put on show. Standing on the boat can be seen the Mayor, John Travis.

Exmoor National Park Authority

This is not really a 'Golden Years' picture as it is too recent, but is a sequel to the previous photograph. It shows the re-enactment of the 'overland launch' in 1999 – the centenary of the original launch. Here the Louisa II *is being manhandled over the cattle grid at the top of Porlock Hill.*

Exmoor National Park Authority

In 1969 there were big celebrations for the centenary of the publication of Lorna Doone, *including a pageant in the Valley of Rocks, following on from a film of the novel being shot locally in 1963. There were many subsequent attempts to keep the* Lorna Doone *connection alive to boost tourism, including 'Doone Days'. Here Doone Day activities take place outside the Lyn and Exmoor Museum in 1978.*

CHAPTER FIVE
❧ A HARD ROAD TO CLIMB ❧

Around Lynton and Lynmouth are some of the steepest stretches of highway in Britain. Local roads were noted for their difficulty well before the days of motor cars. Warner, speaking of Countisbury Hill in 1799, complained that the road did not even have a rail to prevent travellers coming to grief when it was dark. There were several reports from the nineteenth century of horses and carriages falling over the cliff, and even of donkeys missing their footing and carrying passengers to their deaths. Before Lynmouth Hill was built there was only the zigzag path up to Lynton. Being too steep for horses, early visitors were literally manhandled up the hill or paid 6d. for a donkey ride. When Mr Sanford came to take up residence at Clooneavin in 1824 his horses could not pull his carriage up the hill and the carriage itself was carried up by a group of men. After that he put his own money into the improvement of local roads.

In 1894 it was reckoned that nearly 35,000 visitors were taken in and out of Lynton by horse-drawn carriage. At that time the Lynton hotels would tout for business by offering horses to drag their visitors' carriages up the hill from Lynmouth. The first motor car arrived in Lynmouth in 1901, taking an hour and twenty-five minutes to make the journey from Minehead and in 1903 Sir George Newnes became the first resident to have a car. By that year there was already concern about the number of crashes, particularly on Countisbury Hill. It was argued that neither the roads were fit for the cars nor the cars for the roads. In 1903 locals called for cars to be banned from Countisbury Hill and they were backed by the Barnstaple Rural District Council. Hoteliers, however, successfully defeated the proposal as they felt that it would deter wealthier customers from visiting the area. By 1906 most of the local hotels were providing garages. Tom Jones, proprietor of horse-drawn carriages, now also provided charabancs, garaging and petrol. By this time Countisbury Hill had become infamous as the most dangerous hill in the country. Not only that, but many cars which had safely made the descent could not make it up Lynmouth Hill. The cliff railway often had to carry them up, at the considerable cost of between 7s. 6d. and 10s., which compared with the passenger cost of 3d.

Countisbury Hill was very narrow and there was no bank on the cliff side until well into the twentieth century. Early motor coaches could not pass one another along most of its length and would often have to back up for long distances. Here is an early attempt to widen the road at its junction with the drive to the Tors Hotel. The upper part of the hill was not widened until after the flood and even in the 1950s the road was not wide enough for vehicles to pass in places, causing large traffic jams as vehicles reversed up.

John Pedder

The gradient signs on the hill were changed from 1:4 to 25 per cent and this was said to be responsible for a spate of crashes, owing to motorists not fully realising how steep the hill was. The local council protested, to no avail, and eventually erected its own sign in 1967.

A 1930s' Austin Ten crashes on Countisbury Hill in 1945.

Dr M Nightingale

John Pedder

Firemen are called out to a car crash on Countisbury Hill in the 1960s.

In response to the 1903 proposal to ban cars from Countisbury Hill, the Council joined forces with others to improve the Minehead to Lynton road via Dunster, Exford and Simonsbath. Unfortunately, it included the notorious Beggar's Roost hill near Barbrook, which was even steeper than the hills the road was trying to avoid. Beggar's Roost became a challenge for cars and, therefore an attraction for motorists trying to show off new cars. Almost immediately there were fatal crashes and after the First World War the Lynton Urban District Council created a bypass, which meant that motorists arriving at Lynmouth could choose between the 6-mile narrow, steep and winding road to Lynton and the half-mile precipitous route up Lynmouth Hill.

From a local postcard

The original road at Beggar's Roost in the 1940s.

John Pedder

The alternative to Lynmouth Hill was a pretty poor one. Watersmeet Road was, and still is, narrow in places despite continual improvements, and is much prone to landslipping. This car left the A39 along Watersmeet Road in the 1960s and crashed through the wall above Lynrock Bridge, dropping about 100 feet before it was caught by a tree. Miraculously, the driver, Joan Berry, survived.

A group of holidaymakers from Sheffield were injured in June 1952 when their Austin Seven went out of control on Lynmouth Hill and crashed into the barrier at Prospect Corner. PC Pavey gave assistance.

Dr Nightingale treated the injured on the spot and they were taken to Lynton Hospital. The driver, Edrick Shelton, and his wife were detained in hospital, whilst their passengers left after treatment.

This car managed to crash on the relatively gentle part of Lynmouth Hill at Directions Corner in the 1960s, and hung over the crash barrier on to the steep part of the hill.

Horse-drawn coaches continued regular services until 1920 – the last in the country. When Lynmouth Hill was tarmacked, one side was left untouched so that the horse-drawn carriages with removable skids for brakes could grip the road. The coming of the railway in 1898 put paid to services on the Barnstaple run but frequent services continued on the Minehead route up until 1913, when 30 horses were still employed. Beggar's Roost continued to be used for motor sport.

After the new road was constructed it was not necessary to use the cliff railway for carrying cars up to Lynton but some continued to use it to save wear on their tyres. It came into its own again just after the flood disaster, from which it escaped unscathed. As the road to Lynton was blocked, the railway took stranded and wrecked cars up to Lynton. A total of 173 cars were recovered in various states, 52 of which were write-offs, while 38 were never recovered. Pictures of a battered Jowett Javelin car stranded on the parapet of Lyndale Bridge with the bonnet up appeared in newspapers all around the world. It was a brand new motor car and the bonnet was up because the owner had wanted to drive it home the day after the flood and had called out the AA to have a look at it. They duly obliged but could do little to assist! It is interesting that, of the 165 cars reported missing to the RAC, only two were of foreign manufacture – most cars on the roads then were British. Few private vehicles were built during the war and many of the cars on the roads were pre-war but amongst those wrecked were some brand new ones.

After the disaster many lorries were needed to bring heavy supplies to Lynmouth. They could use Lynmouth and Countisbury Hills, although for a few weeks the two were not connected, and, predictably, there were several crashes. Many experienced drivers were needed to negotiate the steep hills with heavy lorries. Army units throughout the country sent excavators and bulldozers; some trailers and their loads weighed up to 50 tons. No loads of such weight had ever negotiated Lynmouth Hill. Each Scammel lorry took an hour to descend the hill, often at night to avoid disrupting traffic during the day. Lorries were often chained together on the hills, with one there just to provide extra brakes. Despite this, on Countisbury Hill one went out of control, crossed Lyndale Bridge and smashed to pieces the new wooden footbridge which had been constructed to span the gap caused by the flood.

A lorry smashes through the parapet of the old Lyndale Bridge in 1954.

An Army vehicle somes to grief at Lynbridge in 1952.

This wartime British Road Services Vulcan crashed at the foot of Lynmouth Hill in 1957.

The same British Road Services lorry appears to have overturned and flipped into the entrance to Glen Lyn, taking no notice of the parking restriction!

A big transporter crashes on the A39 above Dean Steep in 1952.

A Bedford truck beginning the arduous ascent of Lynmouth Hill in 1957.

A Schweppes International lorry hits the safety barrier on Prospect Corner at the bottom of Lynmouth Hill in the late 1950s and gives a new perspective on the term 'mixers'.

The Schweppes lorry is righted by a local breakdown truck.

By the 1950s traffic was becoming heavy in Lynton and Lynmouth and there was only on-street parking. Local councillors Sidney Willshire and 'Jack' Pedder were friendly with the CO of the Marines' amphibious training establishment at Instow. Sidney, a greengrocer, was playing golf with the CO and mentioned that he would like to level Bottom Meadow for a car park. The CO offered to do this as a training exercise for his men. The site was duly levelled at a total cost of £33, which was to cover accommodation of the men who drove the bulldozers.

An Army bulldozer levelling Bottom Meadow for a car park in 1952.

Supervising the building of Bottom Meadow car park in 1952. From left to right: Sidney Willshire, 'Jack' Pedder and Fred Gibbs, the local surveyor.

Following the flood disaster, money was made available not only for much-needed road repairs but also for the improvement of the road infrastructure. There were many improvements to the A39, including three new bridges and road widening. The only hill to be made less steep, however, was Dean Steep at Barbrook.

Soon after the flood, in January 1953, the old railway bridge at the top of Dean Steep was removed and the railway cutting filled in to widen the road.

The old road at the lower part of Dean Steep had run closer to the West Lyn before ascending very steeply to a sharp bend. In 1959 a cutting was made at a higher level to reduce the gradient and make a broader bend. The cutting later became a geological Site of Special Scientific Interest for the sequence of Devonian rocks that it exposed.

The difference between the old and new gradient of Dean Steep can clearly be seen in this picture.

Numbers of visitors and summer traffic were at their height in the early 1970s. Luckily for Exmoor, the A361 North Devon Link Road has taken much of the heavy traffic away from it. In 1975 it was suggested that a scheme for a cable running from Lynmouth to Summerhouse Hill and costing nearly half a million pounds would be the solution to Lynmouth's traffic problems. But they still exist today, with little space for new car parks; the solution is to make best use of existing space.

Exmoor National Park Authority

This coach bringing a party from Curry Rivel, Somerset, in the summer of 1984 had just come over the brow of Station Hill when its brakes failed. It smashed through the wall at the sharp bend at the bottom, on to the top of the tennis courts. Although one passenger was catapulted through the windscreen and there were several injuries, amazingly, no one was killed.

The last three pictures are just to show that motoring was not all fraught with problems. The scenery and the relatively slow speed of the traffic could actually make motoring around Lynton and Lynmouth very pleasurable.

Dr M Nightingale

Dr Nightingale's Standard tourer outside the old station. This was the car in which the doctor would make his rounds into the Exmoor countryside.

Filling up at Elliott's Garage in 1953, when petrol was 4s. 4d. per gallon – less than 22p in today's money. Elliott's Garage grew out of the carriage works of Elliott & Gammon on Cross Street. Prideaux's Garage opened next to the Cottage Hospital in Lee Road in 1910. It later established much larger premises further up the road and eventually took over Elliott's business.

The horse-drawn coach Lorna Doone *was made at Elliott & Gammon's and after going out of service was kept at the bus station on Lee Road, where it made a useful collection box for charities. It is brought out of retirement for special occasions, as here, in May 1988, when it made a number of runs from the Town Hall along Lee Road to the Valley of Rocks and back. This proved very popular with both locals and visitors and in recent years horse-drawn carriage rides have returned.*

CHAPTER SIX
❧ SNOW AND STORM ❧

The Exmoor coast is relatively sheltered from the prevailing southwesterly winds by its high moors and cliffs. The occasional westerly and northwesterly gales can, however, cause problems for coastal settlements, especially if they back high tides. Snow is also not particularly common on the coast as the sea warms the air in winter. However, whilst today it is unusual to have heavy snow at all, in the 'Golden Years' it would be unusual if there was not at least one heavy fall in a winter, especially inland from the A39, which is often the snowline. This made it difficult to sort pictures which were undated. It is clear that there were exceptional winters in 1947, 1963 and 1978 but a snow scene could be almost any winter. Heavy rain, of course, is also not unusual and, again, there was flooding most winters. The disaster of 1952 was not even in winter and a picture of a flood could have been taken at almost any time.

The earliest snow picture in this collection is dated 1940 and shows horses being walked along Station Hill. Hollerday Hill can be seen is in the background.

There was a very severe winter in 1945 with up to 28 degrees of frost. Roads were blocked with drifts up to 12 feet high and the Army was called in to deliver supplies to some villages. The following set of pictures is from that winter.

A tree has fallen with the weight of snow across Sinai Hill.

Snow in Cross Street.

Dr M Nightingale

Outside the Greenhouse in Lee Road.

A Fordson tractor manages to deliver supplies outside WH Smith's, later to become Pedder's newsagents. Smith's had moved from further up Lee Road.

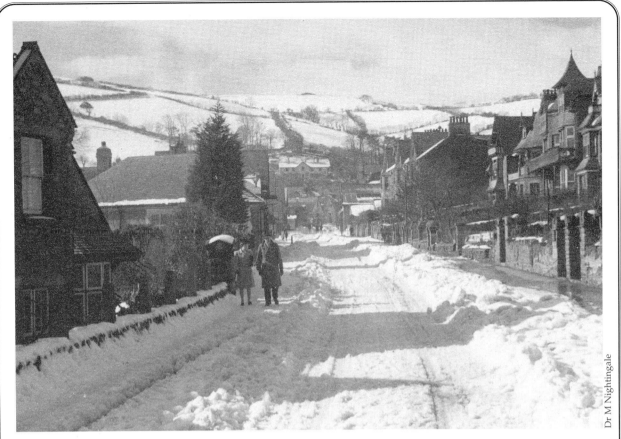

Outside the Cottage Hospital in Lee Road… and care needed to avoid ending up there.

The Methodist Church in Lee Road, beneath a threatening sky.

The memorial outside the Town Hall. Behind is one of the two monkey-puzzle trees that were local landmarks.

More treacherous than usual on Countisbury Hill, thanks to the snow.

Rock House and the Foreland.

The much-photographed Shelley's Cottage at the top of Mars Hill.

In February 1945 Lynton was cut off by snow and as it was wartime there was a labour shortage for clearing it away. This was not automatically carried out by the County Council as nowadays; Lynton and Lynmouth Urban District Council had to foot the bill, having called out a private bulldozer from Woolaways builders in Barnstaple. The following three pictures are dated 1945 but, from the appearance of the vehicles, could well be a few years later.

A man stands on the rear of a van outside St Mary's church to provide more traction.

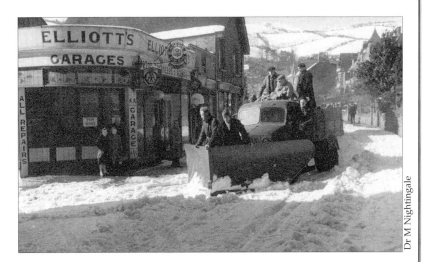

A snowplough outside Elliott's Garage in Lee Road.

The snowplough cutting a swathe down Cross Street.

In many narrow lanes without verges there was the added problem of there being nowhere for snowploughs to push the snow to. Only in recent years have there been blowers which can lift it over the banks. The only alternative until then was the laborious method of shovelling it away by hand.

The first three months of 1947 brought the worst weather conditions recorded since 1881, and for many locals this was the worst winter ever. It was certainly a colder and longer freeze-up even than that of 1963. There were 42 days of frost, with violent blizzards on 28 January, 23 February and 4 March. A snowplough was lost under 10 feet of snow at Lynton. There were fewer snowploughs available than there would be in 1963 but there were still prisoners of war around who could be used to shovel snow from the roads. At Challacombe doctors used skis and horses to get to a woman giving birth. The main roads took so long to be cleared by hand that by the time they were cleared another blizzard would cover them. Workmen complained that it was so cold that icicles hung from their faces, yet still they were criticised for not keeping the roads open. At times there were 13 degrees of frost. Rabbits froze by the roadside, rivers and the sea iced over and frozen seagulls were washed in by the tide. Milk froze in the churns and farmers lost from 20 to 60 per cent of their sheep, according to the altitude of their land. To add to the misery there was freezing rain and mist that coated everything in ice. Telegraph poles doubled their thickness and electricity cables were covered to up to six inches in diameter.

Outside St Mary's church, c.1950.

Lyndale Hotel and Bridge, c.1950.

The Lynton and Barnstaple narrow-gauge railway ran from 1898 until 1935. It was closed because too many people had started to arrive by motor transport instead. This is a view of the old station c.1950, by which time it had become a house. Outside, next to the doctor's car, stands Gladys Edmonds, who lived there until 1979, when Bill Pryor came.

Children playing outside the station in 1950.

Sheep on the A39 c.1950. Winters were always a problem for farmers on high ground. Sheep would shelter under the hedgebanks just where the snow drifted and they often had to be dug out. This farmer is clearly moving his sheep down to lower ground.

Winter is always a time of illness and the doctor often had to make Herculean efforts to carry out his rounds. Cars tended to be rear-wheel drive, and most locals made sure of carrying something heavy in their boot in winter, along with shovels and snow chains. This is the doctor's Standard tourer on the A39 in 1950.

Most winters in the 1950s were hard ones but summers were generally good. A serious freeze-up in February 1954 saw rivers ice over and the A39 blocked with snow drifts.

The doctor's car is blocked by serious snow drifts along the A39 towards Porlock in 1954. The old Standard has now been replaced with a Wolseley.

A snowplough has now been through and piled the snow high on the verge.

Rime, known locally as 'ammil', is unusual nowadays but was once common. The weight of ice was often responsible for bringing down power cables and telephone lines. Telegraph poles with many lines disfigured most main roads in the 'Golden Years' but at least the ammil added some beauty. This picture was taken in 1955; the last big freeze of this sort was in January 1981.

In 1962/63 the snow came in four main doses from late December to early February. It was accompanied by driving wind and there were huge drifts. On the A39 between Lynmouth and Porlock these reached 16 feet deep and snowploughs had to be brought in from other counties to attempt to clear them. Following the snow came a great freeze-up which brought down power cables and crippled water mains. Fuel shortages became as much of a crisis as food supplies.

Outside the Cottage Hospital in Lee Road in the winter of 1963.

Looking over Lee Bay from Lee Abbey, probably in the winter of 1963.

A relief helicopter lands in Bottom Meadow car park in 1963. Lynton and Lynmouth were immediately and completely cut off by snow and there were food shortages within three days. Helicopters from RAF Chivenor were sent for and their first drop consisted of 1300 loaves. After the second fall, on 3 January, the helicopters operated daily.

John Pedder

John Pedder

Another major snowstorm occurred in February 1978. The snow did not last as long as in some winters but it was very deep and in narrow lanes it stayed for many weeks. This picture taken outside St Mary's church is possibly from that winter.

Dr M Nightingale

Sea mists are a common feature of the area and, although a problem for shipping, can be very attractive when viewed from above. They are common in summer when warm air condenses over a cooler sea. This view over the West Lyn valley was taken from Beggar's Roost in 1952.

Many of the businesses along Lynmouth's Esplanade are both barricaded and sandbagged against rough seas in the winter. Special care is also taken against the highest spring tides in April and September. The worst damage is usually when these are backed by westerly gales. Boulders have now been placed against the sea wall to reduce some of the wave damage but it is still quite common for large pebbles to be thrown over the wall by waves and the Esplanade is sometimes not the best place to park a car. In 1956 a freak storm destroyed many fishing boats along the North Devon coast. A big waterspout was seen off Lynmouth in 1966 and these are becoming more common as global warming makes the climate less stable.

Dr M Nightingale

Rough seas batter the Esplanade car park in 1950.

Dr M Nightingale

Waves crash over the sea wall in 1962.

In 1967 waves once again smash over the pier and a very high tide almost laps over the harbour wall.

Floods are not infrequent on the Lyn rivers; in the upper reaches the banks may be overtopped between five and 25 times a year. The problem is thought to have become more frequent since 1947, when farmers started to receive grants for drainage and run-off became more rapid. The worst recorded floods before 1952 were in 1607 and 1769 but other severe spells, such as in 1947, meant locals grew well used to them, causing an added problem in 1952. Householders were loathe to evacuate their houses, thinking that it would be not be any more than a 'normal' flood. The following pictures were taken in the 1940s.

The East Lyn from Lyndale Bridge, with the balconies of the Lyndale Hotel on the right.

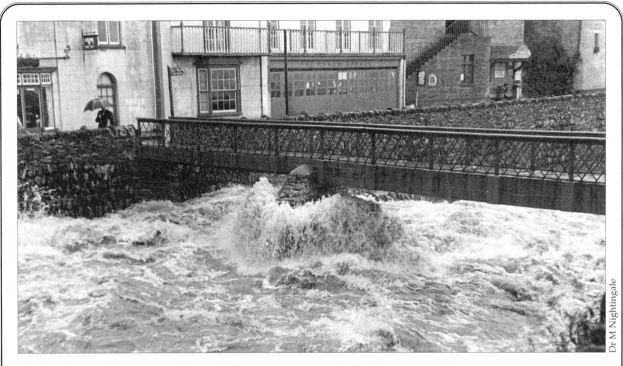

The Lyn batters the support of the footbridge running across to the Manor grounds.

A 'training arm' was designed to keep the flooding river away from boats in the harbour. This had little effect in 1952, and afterwards it was rebuilt much larger and stronger.

The West Lyn was confined to a narrow channel between the West Lyn Café and Lyn Valley Hotel. The bridge here took Lynmouth Street over the river and was an early casualty in the 1952 flood, along with the side of the Lyn Valley Hotel.

A view of the West Lyn from Prospect Bridge upstream from the former picture.

The West Lyn cuts across a meander above Barbrook.

The whole of 1952 saw extreme weather, apart from the flood in August. In January a gale blew a roof off in Lynmouth, and this was followed by a severe snowstorm. In April heavy rain made the road subside at Directions Corner, and a thunderstorm in July caused flooding in Lynton and Lynmouth. From then until the disaster it continued to be unusually wet for the time of year. Only a week after the flood yet another thunderstorm caused more flooding, cutting off newly restored power. In December, with a blizzard and the threat of subsequent snow melt, the prospect loomed again. In the event, flooding occurred elsewhere but it was a storm which caused more disruption to Lynmouth. Over the next few years reconstruction efforts were hampered by further flooding, which damaged or wrecked temporary structures.

This picture shows scaffolding along the bank of the East Lyn at Tors Road. This had been been erected to hold shuttering in which to pour concrete for the support for the road. A temporary bridge had been made to carry the concrete across the river from the car park where it was being mixed. A flood in September 1953 demolished the bridge.

The same bridge, looking downstream.

A new channel for the Lyn was created by cutting away the road and buildings on the Manor Green side of the river. This was just being completed when a flood in March 1954 washed away the temporary bank holding the river in its former course.

There was a further damaging flood in October 1954. Here the West Lyn is seen in spate below Barbrook.

During the 1952 flood the West Lyn had changed course, cutting a deep new channel down the road alongside Lyndale Bridge. The channel was quickly filled in after the flood so that the road could be reopened. The filling was of loose gravel and boulders and the side of the road was easily cut away by the 1954 flood.

The same scene as before, showing the collapse of the road beside Lyndale Bridge a few weeks before the bridge was rebuilt.

There have been many floods since 1954 but nothing quite as bad as in 1952. In 1958 the Lyn rivers came to be bank-full in places; 1960 saw flooding throughout North Devon and recurrences in 1978 and 1982 were severe enough for people to be evacuated from their properties on the East Lyn, from Watersmeet upwards.

CHAPTER SEVEN
❦ THE AFTERMATH ❦

Pictures of the disaster as it took place on 15 August 1952 are not available as the worst of it happened at night. However, many pictures were taken of the damage next day and the day after that and these hit the front pages of newspapers all over the country. The following are pictures taken by the doctor during rescue operations the day after. Much of the rescue work had, however, taken place during the night and the day after was spent mainly treating the injured, evacuating residents and visitors and finding bodies.

A St John Ambulance Service first-aid post, manned by local volunteers was quickly set up at Lynmouth and stayed for a month, dealing with hundreds of minor injuries.

Locals survey the cause of much of the damage. Tree trunks had blocked Prospect Bridge at the foot of Lynmouth Hill and the West Lyn was diverted to the south, cutting across the road and destroying many buildings in its new course towards the East Lyn.

Police remove a body from the wreckage of buildings.

Dr M Nightingale

The new course of the West Lyn.

Looking up Watersmeet Road, blocked by a huge pile of debris.

Dr M Nightingale

The Lyndale Hotel was at the centre of destruction but, remarkably, survived. Access to it across the West Lyn was not possible until temporary footbridges were erected. The watermark left by the flood can be seen just below the top-floor windows.

Much of the present Lynmouth Street was flooded but escaped serious damage. On the outside of the bend in the river, however, its bank was undercut. To the right of this picture are the remains of the Beach Hotel. The manageress and 13 guests had climbed on to the roof during the flood and were rescued with a ladder dropped from Mars Hill behind. Shortly after the last guest had climbed to safety the hotel collapsed.

Looking over Lynmouth Street towards the sea. The harbour is filled with tree trunks and debris, the end of the pier has gone, and the Rhenish Tower with it, but, surprisingly, not the deckchairs piled to the inside of the tower. To the left is a gap where the Beach Hotel had stood and beyond it the remains of the former lifeboat house.

An assortment of wreckage on the beach in front of Rock House. Across the river can be seen the remains of the lifeboat house.

Boulders from the West Lyn block Lynmouth Street in front of the Lyn Valley Hotel. Behind the rubble is Island Cottage.

There were about a thousand residents and a similar number of visitors in Lynmouth on the night of the disaster. In all about 1500 were evacuated during 16 August. Many went to rest centres set up in Minehead and Lynton and friends and relatives in Lynton and the surrounding area put up many others.

By 17 August work started on clearing some of the debris from the roads to make it possible for heavy transporters to arrive with bulldozers and excavators.

This picture shows the former course of the West Lyn below Prospect Bridge, with the Falls and Granville House hotels behind. The large boulder right of centre was estimated to weigh 50 tons. Such boulders could not be moved and workmen from Devon County Council had to blast them with dynamite.

This shows the destruction caused by the West Lyn before its course had been diverted. It used to come out between the West Lyn Hotel and Café and the Lyn Valley Hotel, which has partly collapsed. There is no sign of the bridge which had carried Lynmouth Street over the river.

As the tide went out servicemen had the grim task of searching for bodies on the foreshore.

The shore in front of the Manor Green was littered with cars and all kinds of wreckage from houses and hotels, but mostly with wood – boards, furniture and trees which had been swept down the gorges. Some stood like a petrified forest. For weeks afterwards this floating debris came and went with the tide. Much of the wreckage and some bodies were carried down the coast, one victim even being found beyond Clovelly.

The Glen Lyn Garage at the foot of Lynmouth Hill had two large petrol storage tanks under its forecourt. It was feared that they would pose a danger to workers clearing the debris. As it happened, the petrol station had completely disappeared in the flood, tanks included. The petrol pumps, however, appeared later on the beach.

Four days after the disaster Harold Macmillan, then Minister for Housing and Local Government, visited Lynmouth. In a national broadcast he set out a three-phase recovery plan: immediate relief to affected people, temporary reconstruction and permanent reconstruction.

For Phase 1 there was much immediate assistance from police, fire brigade, armed services, council workmen and voluntary services. Clothing, food and shelter came immediately. Earl Fortescue and Lord Hylton, the Lords Lieutenant of Devon and Somerset launched an appeal two days after the disaster, setting up a fund called the North Devon and West Somerset Flood Relief Fund. This was administered by the National Provincial Bank in Exeter, who were themselves deluged by the response. From all over Britain and around the world up to nearly £100,000 a day arrived and by October over £1m had been raised. The fund stayed open and when it closed four years later nearly another £400,000 had been added, including a Government contribution of £25,000. In all, money was given to 1710 people who had suffered losses. The sum of £27,000 was spent on the rebuilding of private roads, bridges and river walls. The fund still exists and, the remaining money being invested, the trustees meet twice a year to distribute roughly £6000 interest to causes throughout the area affected by the flooding. The last widow to receive a pension from the fund died in the 1980s.

After the rescue of people trapped by the flood was completed, clearing up began astonishingly rapidly. Phase 2 involved the excavation and removal of hundreds of thousands of tons of debris and boulders from streets and rivers, erecting temporary Bailey bridges and supporting or demolishing dangerous buildings. Working day and night, hundreds of workmen managed to achieve this in one month, despite an initial estimate of six months. Some water and telephone services were restored within days, along with the construction of footbridges. The Barnstaple firm of Woolaways and other building contractors were fully occupied. Part of Lynton and Lynmouth had been supplied by Lynmouth's own hydro-electric power station, which had been put out of action by the flood and work to connect the area to the National Grid was hastily completed.

Armed service personnel stationed throughout the West Country were quickly on the scene. An equipment depot was set up at Blackmoor Gate, complete with NAAFI. They were mostly accommodated in hotels in Lynton but also set up a camp and workshops here at Bottom Meadow car park in Lynton. Major General Firbank and Field Marshal Slim few into the car park by helicopter to agree an action plan and at the height of operations over 1000 servicemen were involved.

Some of the relief workers were encamped either side of the cricket ground in the Valley of Rocks.

Here the troops have erected temporary footbridges to span the new course of the West Lyn and link what had become three separated parts of Lynmouth. The bridge in the foreground linked to Lyndale Bridge so that supplies could be brought in from the Countisbury side. However, it was soon demolished by an Army lorry that went out of control. Within another couple of days they had erected a Bailey bridge at Barbrook, reconnecting the main road from Barnstaple to Lynmouth.

Dr M Nightingale

High priority was to restore the road from Lyndale Bridge to the bottom of Lynmouth Hill. To do this it was necessary to take the West Lyn back to something like its former course. Here an Army bulldozer has started to clear the new channel.

Dr M Nightingale

The West Lyn had created its own delta where it joined the East Lyn, which in turn had been forced eastwards to undercut the road to Rock House. This had to be cut through to create the new channel.

When the new channel was created bulldozers quickly filled in the deep chasm the West Lyn had cut through the road next to Lyndale Bridge.

There was a race against time to build up the river banks as protection from the high spring tides in September.

Much debris from the flood was carried out to sea but that left in the river channels had raised their beds by 6–10 feet and at Lynmouth 70,000 cubic yards of material had to be removed. An idea to tip it all on the moor, thankfully, proved too expensive. Most went to extend the Esplanade car park. The Tracto-loader and three bulldozers could not cope with the largest boulders, which had to be blown up. Over the next few months there were thousands of explosions and more damage was caused by rocks falling from them.

Dr M Nightingale

Dr M Nightingale

Most of the servicemen were withdrawn by 11 September, leaving the specialist engineers to work with local council workers and builders. Temporary road bridges were erected over the West Lyn, and Lynmouth Street reopened. Here the road is being cleared in front of the site of the Beach Hotel. Firemen washed down furniture and other belongings and disinfected before locals were allowed to return to salvage them. The village reopened on 16 September.

Some locals who had been rendered homeless by the flood could not return and were given temporary accommodation in caravans adjacent to Holman Park. Six of the caravans were donated by individuals as part of the Relief Fund. The camp was used between August 1952 and March 1953.

A fortnight after the caravan site opened electricity was installed, free of charge, by the South Western Electricity Board.

North Devon Athenaeum

Aid to the victims of the disaster continued in one form or another for weeks, even years afterwards. Here the WVS presents a food parcel to Mrs King in February 1953.

Dr M Nightingale

Weakened by the flood in August, the road at Directions Corner collapsed in November 1952. A few weeks earlier a lorry bringing flood relief had gone over the side into the West Lyn gorge. The landslide took with it the RAC phone box and part of the water pipe supplying the cliff railway. Luckily RB Carnegie, the County Surveyor, was on hand to find a solution, which was to blast a new road out of solid rock.

Dr M Nightingale

There were further small landslides. Members of the local publicity association were annoyed at BBC broadcasts of such problems. Trade was desperately bad and they did not want to put off more people from coming to the area.

Looking down on the council houses at Barbrook c.1954. To the left of the four blocks of semi-detached council houses stood another block which was swept away by the flood. Twelve people lost their lives here, including six members of the Floyd family. In 1954 a memorial garden was built on the site to Australian girls Gwenda Oxley and Joyce Hiscock who died there whilst they were returning to one of the houses where they were guests.

Lynbridge had survived relatively well compared with Barbrook upstream. Ye Olde Cottage Inn had similar supports to the council houses that had been undermined at Barbrook. The bridge next to it was washed away, along with part of the road, washing a car into the river, but the Inn itself survived. The mill downstream survived but its wheel, which had been used for workshop machinery, was finally put out of action.

Dr M Nightingale

Dr M Nightingale

Dr M Nightingale

The Lyndale Hotel had amazingly survived the torrent, considering that it was in the centre of destruction and lay beside where the West Lyn, which had altered its course, joined the East Lyn. Boulders, some of them weighing 15 tons, were piled up against one wall to a depth of 30 feet and at the hotel the East Lyn reached a depth of 60 feet above its normal level. The wreckage of a chapel, fruit shop and garage was smashed against the wall. One wing did succumb but the main building, with many visitors and rescued locals, remained intact. As a final act of the flood, however, the weakened east wing collapsed after heavy rain in July 1954.

CHAPTER EIGHT
❧ RESURGAM ❧

Rebuilding in Lynmouth did not take place until about eighteen months after the flood and took several years to complete. The following sequence of photographs looking down on Lynmouth from Summerhouse Hill probably best illustrates the changes that took place during the 1950s.

This picture of c.1950 shows the harbour with a low pier beyond the Rhenish Tower and a low 'training arm' dividing the harbour from the river. Lynmouth Street is the only route through Lynmouth and buildings line both banks of the river.

Here, in January 1953 the Rhenish tower, training arm and end of the pier have been washed away by the flood. A car park stands in the triangle where a block of buildings was washed away. The east bank of the river and road has been eroded and the mouth of the West Lyn has a temporary bridge.

In April 1954 the Rhenish Tower has been rebuilt and the pier strengthened and extended. The river has been moved eastwards, with buildings and road removed on the east side, to be replaced by a terraced bank and a footpath above. The buildings on the west bank are now set back from the river with a new road, Riverside Road, running in between.

In c.1960 the harbour has been protected from the river by a strengthened and extended training arm. Blocks of buildings either side of the West Lyn have been demolished, the river straightened and its banks widened, as have those of the East Lyn. New, longer and wider bridges have been built over the West and East Lyn rivers. Lyndale Hotel has been demolished and a new coach and car park stands in its place.

The village relied heavily on tourism then as now and was open for business as usual within a few months of the disaster. Residents were allowed to return after a month but there was a ban on visitors for a while longer. Within a fortnight Lynton traders were appealing for it to be lifted. Business was badly hit even though the flood had put the town on the map and many wanted to visit the scene. Major construction works were confined to off-season months but even so, many visitors complained about the noise. It also took a long time to purchase the property needed to widen rivers, create car parks and widen and reroute roads. Negotiations for one road deviation took three-and-a-half years.

Dr M Nightingale

Residents of Lynmouth had been evacuated after the flood, some to Lynton and some to Minehead, because of the risk of disease. Water had to be brought to Lynton by tanker because it was unfit to drink and Lynmouth was without water or sewerage. The smell of sewage was many people's main memory and the repair of broken drains was one of the first priorities before people could be allowed back to their homes. Here a workman gets on with that job in May 1953.

Dr M Nightingale

In the triangle of roads in between which several buildings had been washed away developed a temporary car park, as here in 1953. This was convenient for visitors in the village where parking had been very limited before the flood.

Dr M Nightingale

This picture from 1953 is titled 'Undefeated'. It shows Shelley's Cottage Hotel, damaged by the flood, but open for business as usual.

The following sequence of pictures was taken on the first anniversary of the flood, 15 August 1953. It shows the clearing-up operation nearing completion and Lynmouth prior to rebuilding.

Though a plan for rebuilding the rest of Lynmouth was not in place, it was considered a priority that work should go ahead immediately to rebuild the pier, to protect the harbour and works on the river bank. The pile driving had to take place whenever the tide was low enough, and many visitors were kept awake through the nights.

Work on the harbour slipway.

Workmen stand where the road used to be on the east bank of the river.

Cars park where the Glen Lyn Garage had been.

Visitors stand and survey where the West Lyn had diverted its course and caused much destruction. A new road has now been constructed.

Clearing a new course for the West Lyn was completed within weeks. Now it was time to do the same for the East Lyn.

The Government paid for the rebuilding of public property throughout the Exmoor area, which at Lynmouth itself cost £707,191. Initial estimates put the total recovery cost at £6 million over three years. Work would involve many different agencies: Lynton Urban District Council was responsible for roads, harbour, housing and sewerage; Devon County Council for roads; the Ministry of Housing and Local Government for harbour, housing and sewerage; the Ministry of Transport and Civil Aviation for roads; the Devon River Board and Ministry of Agriculture and Fisheries for rivers; Central Electricity for bringing the National Grid to Lynton and Lynmouth and the North Devon Water Board for the water supply. Devon County Council co-ordinated these agencies.

Three options for the rebuilding of Lynmouth were discussed by interested parties: to tidy up and rebuild much as before but with an effective flood-warning system; to plan for a flood of the same size; to provide the greatest possible safety measures, involving wide rivers, dams and flood channels. Locals felt that they wanted their old Lynmouth back and initially favoured the first option. Many thought that the disaster would never be repeated even though flooding in Lynmouth was common and there had been the devastating examples of 1607 and 1769. It was argued that floods could not be prevented but their effects could be alleviated. The third option proved too costly and would have largely depopulated Lynmouth of both residents and visitors.

The County Council worked up Option 2. The river authorities engaged Mr CH Dobbie to ascertain the volume of the flood and suggest works to contain future floods of similar proportions. Included in his recommendations were: the spans of all bridges; the widths and depths of rivers at Lynmouth, Hillsford Bridge, Barbrook and Parracombe; the construction of traps for boulders on the East and West Lyns; an overflow channel over the Manor Green at Lynmouth. Another idea was to create reservoirs and tunnel an overflow channel under Countisbury Hill from the East Lyn to Sillery Sands. However, it was decided that it was too costly to build and operate the boulder traps and overflow channels. At a public meeting in February 1953 a detailed model of the proposals, drawn up by Devon County Surveyor Mr RB Carnegie, was shown. The opportunity was also taken to design new roads and car parks to cater for the increasing volume of traffic. Assurances were given by the Urban District Council that everything would be rebuilt in local stone and Lynmouth would remain a beautiful place.

The Carnegie plan model for the rebuilding of Lynmouth, 1953.

Dr M Nightingale

Dr M Nightingale

A close-up of the model shows how actual works differed slightly from the plan. The training arm at the harbour was extended further. The bank of the East Lyn was terraced but the bank of the West Lyn was not.

Another view shows the Lyn Valley and Lyndale Hotels retained, whereas they were eventually demolished.

The new channels for the Lyn rivers were widened to accommodate the maximum flow of the flood, as calculated by Dobbie and confirmed by testing models at Imperial College, London. The channel for the combined Lyn rivers was constructed three times as wide as before. In a larger flood it would allow water to spill over Manor Green and be carried away from the village. It was terraced to allow full flow over the river bed in dry spells. The peak flood does not occur at the same time in each river and so the channel for the combined rivers is designed for less than the total for both Lyns but also taking into consideration high tides.

Work began on the bank along Tors Road first, in July 1953, to protect the properties there. The foundations were excavated to bedrock and the walls made of concrete slabs, which replaced the old drystone walling.

The concrete was mixed beside Watersmeet Road and a scaffolding bridge was made to carry it over the river. The concrete was faced with stone 'ditching' made from the remains of blown-up boulders.

The scaffolding bridge was demolished by a further flood in September 1953 but by October it had been rebuilt.

Dr M Nightingale

Work continued over the next three years on the remaining river banks. Here, in October, work has started on removing a large area of the east bank of the Lyn. A temporary footbridge spans the old channel of the river.

Dr M Nightingale

A month later and excavators have reached the level of the new river course.

Work starts on the 'ditching' of the terracing for the new river bank.

In December 1953 work starts on the concrete support for the bank of the new Riverside Road, which was opened in June 1954.

Apart from tidying up the course of the river immediately after the flood, work had not started on the west bank and the balconies at the backs of the apartments along Lynmouth Street still overhung the river as they always had.

In February 1954 the west bank of the new river course is clearly taking shape. The existing course of the river is along where the new road is about to be made.

Because of a flood in March the river prematurely occupies its new channel.

By April the east bank is complete and the river is in its new position, with work running apace on Riverside Road.

Meanwhile, back in August 1953, work continued on excavating the harbour. One of the Ruston Bucyrus excavators broke down and was covered by three high tides before it was rescued.

All new banks and piers were protected against scouring by steel-sheet piles. Most banks were made of reinforced concrete faced with local stone. Here, in October 1953, the new pier begins to take shape.

Dr M Nightingale

By January 1954 the concrete of the pier was being faced with stone.

Dr M Nightingale

Another view in January 1954 showing the steel shuttering for the new harbour wall.

Dr M Nightingale

By March 1954 the new pier was almost complete.

As soon as the pier was finished work started on a replacement for the Rhenish Tower. No plans existed and Blackford's, the contractors, rebuilt it from post-card pictures. The only original part of the tower to be replaced was the fire basket, which was recovered from the foreshore.

By September 1954 the new tower was complete and a familiar landmark once more.

In July 1954 work started on a new training arm to keep the river from the harbour. In the distance can be seen finishing touches to a new causeway beyond the pier. This was partly for steamer passengers to use at low tide and partly to prevent pebbles from the west beach blocking the river mouth.

Within days the training arm takes shape.

Dr M Nightingale

A distant view of work on the training arm shows the new harbour already in use.

North Devon Athenaeum

This undated photograph shows the reopening of the harbour. In the boat are Major Blackhurst, the chairman of the Council. To his right are Town Clerk Leonard Ridge and Jayne Blackhurst, his daughter. The total cost of the rebuilding was nearly £50,000 but £66,000 had been spent to make new sea defences on the West Beach and create a temporary harbour for the 1953 season.

A dozen buildings in Lynmouth were demolished to make way for widening river banks. This added to the 55 demolished by the flood. Although many damaged buildings were repaired, about a quarter of the buildings in Lynmouth were lost and never replaced. Many of the people made homeless were later rehoused in Lynton. Before the disaster the population of Lynmouth was 450 and today it is about 100, although the decline is not all directly related.

In April 1954 work on the riverbank along Tors Road was complete but work on the west bank, including demolition of the old power station, had not started.

In order for Riverside Road to be completed and the Lyndale Bridge extended to meet it, a block of hotels had to be demolished. Here goes the Falls Hotel in May 1954.

The Granville House Hotel is left standing, shortly to follow the Falls.

Much of the demolition work took place in the summer, providing a spectacle for visitors. Here the temporary car park adjacent to the Lyndale Hotel is full of coaches. The Granville House Hotel has gone but the shattered remains of the Lyn Valley Hotel across the West Lyn are still there.

The Lyndale Hotel, which had miraculously survived the flood, stands alone the day before its demolition on August Bank Holiday, 1954.

Dr M Nightingale

A last view of the Lyndale Hotel from the ruins of the neighbouring Lyn Valley Hotel.

Dr M Nightingale

This last shot from the windows of the Lyndale Hotel shows the unfinished area around the river junctions.

Demolition begins on the rear of the Lyndale Hotel.   ...and then on the side...

Demolition is complete by October 1954 and work starts on a permanent course for the West Lyn.

The Lyndale Hotel has gone whilst the old Prospect Bridge remains. The banks of the West Lyn above the bridge have already been widened and the construction of a new bridge is awaited.

Devon County Council continued with work on the roads and bridges. The roads in the outer area were reconstructed first as those in Lynmouth would have to carry heavy construction traffic for some time and new surfacing would be rapidly ruined. There was some argument between the County and Urban District councils over the design of the new bridges. The former argued for flat concrete slab bridges on economic grounds and the latter for stone arches on aesthetic grounds. The argument raged until March 1957 when the Minister was called in and decided in favour of the County. Concrete was in short supply at the time and pre-stressed concrete was the most economical use of materials. The two bridges over the West Lyn at Lynmouth, two at Barbrook and one at Hillsford were among the first of their kind in Britain. The engineering of them became very technical and new ground was broken, arousing much academic interest. They were constructed in small sections, using the same moulds for each bridge to save money. The five bridges cost £162,000. A compromise was reached over Lyndale Bridge, which had a concrete span disguised as a stone arch. Stone facing for that and some concrete footbridges was salvaged from demolished buildings. Wooden footbridges were made to lift off their mountings in a flood so as not to dam the rivers.

Two temporary bridges span the West Lyn in August 1954.

The Lyndale Bridge that was about to be demolished was not the first one to have been on that site. Whilst excavating foundations for a new bridge in December 1954, the foundations of the previous double-arched bridge were found, 12 feet below the existing one.

The old Prospect Bridge withstood the full force of the flood but would have resulted in less damage if it had not. Here, in 1957, it was demolished to make way for a wider concrete bridge.

In November 1957 the Lyn Valley Hotel became the last building to be demolished. A workman watches from one of the new Prospect Bridge.

Two new concrete bridges were built across the much-widened West Lyn channel.

The final moments of the Lyn Valley Hotel.

The hotel was cleared to leave an open space. The Devon Committee of the National Park paid for its maintenance for several years until it was redeveloped.

By the mid-1960s the site had been developed with new shops and apartments.

A view of the new Lyndale and Riverside bridges in the mid-1960s.

Another view from the mid-1960s showing the new footbridge to the Manor Green.

A view of the new Hillsford Bridge on the Hoaroak Water, which had been built at the same time as the West Lyn bridges.

Chiselcombe Bridge on the East Lyn below Watersmeet, a concrete structure faced with stone, was completed in 1957. The concrete was delivered from the road above through a chute of oil drums welded together. The bridge replaced two destroyed by the flood: the original Chiselcombe Bridge 400 yards downstream, just above Myrtleberry, and Bridge Pool Bridge just upstream. It is a high-arched structure built to reach over another flood of 1952 proportions; in a flood of 1982 water came up to the base of the arch but it has yet to be tested.

The official completion of the rebuilding of Lynmouth was marked by the opening of the Flood Memorial Hall on 10 July 1958. The hall, paid for by the Relief Fund, now houses a flood exhibition and replaced the former lifeboat house and Village Institute washed away by the flood. The recovery thus took nearly six years to complete.

CHAPTER NINE
❧ THE LEE ABBEY STORY ❧

The Lee Abbey fellowship is an organisation which grew from Christian holiday house parties organised by Roger de Pemberton, a Cheltenham curate, in the mid-1930s. During the war he sought to use school premises for these house parties in summer holidays. At that time Lee Abbey was used by a private school. Roger had known it when it was an hotel before the war and saw that it was a suitable place because of its tranquil and beautiful setting. He used it for August house parties from 1943 and Easter gatherings from 1945. In that year a group of clergy formed the Pathfinder Trust, named after the *Pathfinder* magazine in which the house parties were advertised. The Trust decided to purchase Lee Abbey as a permanent centre for such activities.

A view of Lee Abbey in the early 1950s.

Lee Abbey became an hotel in 1921 upon the death of its owner, Charles Bailey. The hotel spent much money on bedroom accommodation, hydro-electric power, tennis courts, a café and the creation of a golf course in front of the house but the economic climate at the time was not good and by the time of the Second World War it had become run down. War put an end to visitors, forcing the hotel into bankruptcy.

The north side of the Abbey in 1949.

After Dunkirk many schools from the southeast of England were evacuated, their own premises being commandeered by the Army. From 1940 Lee Abbey became home for Brambletye Preparatory School from East Grinstead in Sussex, who moved there lock, stock and barrel with all of their furniture and equipment and what remained of their teaching and domestic staff. The building was covered with camouflage paint lest German bombers returning from raids on South Wales chose to jettison any remaining bombs on important-looking buildings. The school remained until September 1945, when the Pathfinder Trust took over the building. They did nothing to maintain the building and the only sign of their occupancy is graffiti scratched on window panes, including 'Hamilton is a wet' and 'Miss Snooks is a wet'.

The west front of the buildings in 1953.

One of the first house parties in 1946, when the house was still covered with camouflage paint.

When the Pathfinder Trust took over the Abbey after the war the buildings were very dilapidated. Much needed replacing and there were shortages of labour and materials, let alone the money to pay for them. The Trust relied heavily on self-help and gifts. Not only were there buildings but also a 350-acre estate to run.

After a year of work on the buildings, the Abbey was furnished and habitable by June 1946, when the first post-war house party took place. 'An opening Conference and Dedication for those actively interested in Evangelism and Lee Abbey' was the title for this first programme. The Dedication was on 5 June, a gloriously sunny day amidst a wet week. A procession was led by Charles Curzon, the Bishop of Exeter, plus the Archdeacon of Barnstaple, Rector of Lynton and many other clergy, trustees and conference guests. Singing hymns as it went, the party wound its way in and out of the buildings, stopping to dedicate the chapel, lounge, workshops and land.

Summer 1946 continued with house parties for different types of people such as foreign visitors, youth groups and young married couples. Although the Trust was run by Anglicans, the house parties were open to all Christian denominations. In the winter the Trust put together a staff to run the estate and organise the gatherings. Leslie Sutton had done much of the organising until then, when Roger de Pemberton became the first warden and many people came to work as part of the community. Roger left in 1950 when there was a split between the work of the Pathfinder Trust, which continued work nationwide, and the Council of the Abbey. The Council itself later had nationwide branches, encompassed under the Lee Abbey Fellowship.

The dedication procession in 1946, with the Bishop of Exeter following the crosier.

The small lounge in 1950.

Farewell to guests in the 1960s.

House party guests leaving in 1956.

The winter of 1946/47 was the hardest for over fifty years. Lee Abbey was still not well furbished but it had its own hydro-electric and diesel generators for electricity, and woodland for firewood. It was cut off by snow for several weeks and residents had to drag sledges to Lynton and back for supplies. Added to the difficulties, an outbreak of flu affected most of the residents and staff. The Community at the Abbey gradually built up to about 60; while most stay for a year or two, others are seasonal or stay for many years.

Lee Abbey Community in 1953.

The Community in 1955.

The story of Lee Abbey has been one of constant building and improvement. In 1955, 12 single rooms were provided in an annexe at the rear of the main house. In 1957 Garden Lodge was built to accommodate the warden and his family away from the main house, and in 1959 two bungalows were added for chaplains. In 1966 six single rooms for men were built in the walled garden. In the 1980s many Community members were given new accommodation when the 'rabbit hutches' and 'stables' built to house hotel staff temporarily in the 1920s were replaced. A sports hall was built at the same time.

Building work in progress 1953.

Much work on the estate was undertaken by volunteers. Every Easter from 1948 there were fortnightly student working parties staying at the Abbey, drawing particularly on Oxford and Cambridge universities.

A student work party in 1957.

The original chapel at the Abbey was in Squire Bailey's bedroom. It was a large, light and airy room and eminently suitable except that it could only hold 40 people and the Community had risen to about 80, without guests. The only answer was to build a new chapel but after the war there was a shortage of building materials, which meant that a licence was required for new religious buildings, and that was not granted. In 1951 Warden Geoffrey Rogers and Estate Manager Geoffrey Hutchison decided to knock three bedrooms into one room which could seat a hundred people. The demolition work was done by a student work party, the carpentry by the Community and the plastering by a local builder, and the project was completed in a few weeks.

Converting bedrooms into the new chapel in 1952.

The twenty-first anniversary of the Abbey came in 1967 and was accompanied by further building work. Until then service vehicles had to drive all around the front of the house to the yard at the rear but now new road provided direct access to the yard. Also built were a new bedroom block, playroom and laundry for guests.

Wardens Ken Pillar and Madeline Wheen receiving giant 'keys to the door' at the twenty-first anniversary celebrations. Madeline was Lady Warden for twenty-eight years, working alongside the Warden, who has always been male.

Lee Abbey in the 1960s showing the access road around the front of the building.

Another picture from the 1960s showing access to the car park at the rear of the building.

Lee Abbey developed close links with churches abroad and in September 1951, on the recommendation of a Dutch pastor, Princess Wilhelmina of Holland joined a house party at the Abbey. During the war she had been Queen of the Netherlands but had abdicated in favour of her daughter. The Abbey still being far from luxurious, the princess stayed at the Tors Hotel at Lynmouth and took a local taxi to the Abbey each day. She took communion in the Anglican Church for the first time and planted a pine tree in memory of her visit.

Princess Wilhelmina planting a tree in memory of her visit in 1951.

The building on top of the limekiln at Lee Bay was built as a beach café when the Abbey was an hotel in the 1920s. After the hotel closed the café became vandalised. On 15 August 1952, the Youth Camp in a field nearby was becoming washed out and winds were tearing at the tents, so the girls camped in the old café whilst the boys huddled together in the main marquee. David Cole, a member of the Community had brought his car down to the beach road to help take some of the wet bedding up to the house to dry. As he returned to the car he was swept down the road by the Lee Stream. Only by hanging on to a gatepost by Pelton House, 50 yards downstream, was he able to save himself. Elsie Savill, the camp quartermaster, followed him shortly and was also lucky to save herself from being washed out to sea.

By 3am the river had reached the door of the beach café but, luckily, never reached the girls inside. The next morning there was a 10-feet-deep trench where the road had been. A massive tree trunk had wedged across the stream and deflected the water from the café. Some of the girls had even managed to have a good night's sleep, whilst the boys in the field above had spent a wet night trying to stop their tents from blowing away. Although most roads were blocked, half of the road at Barbrook was still open and three coaches were brought in to take guests away from the Abbey. Luckily, however, the Abbey's own water and electricity supplies were still functioning and it escaped relatively lightly compared with Lynmouth. For a while the road past the Abbey was the main route into Lynton.

The beach café surounded by debris after the flood disaster in August 1952.

The beach café was later restored by the Lee Abbey Community as a chalet for guests. In the 1960s a tractor fell down the cliff towards a group of people by the chalet. Those people say that they saw an angel guide it away from them; the incident was recreated for a recent television programme. Ley Chapel was built in the limekiln underneath the chalet in the 1980s by Stan Gorton, the Building and Maintenance Manager on the estate. He cleared out the eighteenth-century limekiln below the beach c halet and made the pews himself from wood on the estate.

The estate had 190 acres of woodland and 60 acres of pasture on the former golf course in front of the house and on Crock Point. A further 100 acres of pasture around another golf course at Caffyns Down was sold off in 1951 to help pay the mortgage on the estate. The woodland on the estate had not been maintained since Lee Abbey had been a private house and the Community spent much effort in clearing footpaths through it and creating tranquil walks for guests. Many trees fell in winter gales, and much of the old oak woodland on Duty Point came down in a hurricane in December 1981. A long-term plan involving thinning and replanting was then worked out with assistance from the National Park Authority.

The Lee Abbey dairy herd started with eight Welsh Black cows and a calf in 1948. The Welsh Blacks were very hardy and good milkers, producing milk and clotted cream for the Community and guests but as the farmland was improved they were replaced with Ayrshires in 1955. Friesians were added later, making a milking herd of up to 40 cattle.

Calves in the field next to the tea garden in the 1950s.

Cattle passing the tea garden on the way to milking in 1955.

Meadows on the former golf course in 1955.

Foot and Mouth disease struck Lynton in 1958. At that time it was only infected cattle which were destroyed and the Lee Abbey herd was not affected. In 1990 2½ acres were added to provide additional spring water for the estate. Silage and hay were made to feed the cattle, but feed and straw also had to be bought in.

A frozen drinking trough in 1956.

Cattle behind the house in 1957.

Cutting grass for hay in the 1950s.

Cattle passing haystacks in 1956.

Haymaking in 1957.

A break for haymakers in 1957.

In 1967 a generous gift was made to the Abbey to make the Community more self-sufficient and it was used for new farm buildings. John Burkett, architect of the award-winning new bedroom block in 1968 was employed and the new farm buildings, built a year later on the former guest car park, also won an award. They enabled the dairy herd to be doubled in size and more efficiently fed and milked.

The old milking parlour.

The award-winning bedroom wing seen to the left of the tower in the 1970s.

The herd was sold in 1992 under a reorganisation of the estate by Warden Mike Edson. Although still profitable (providing for the Abbey's needs and making a profit of £1000 per annum on the surplus), the dairy herd and market garden were seen to be taking up too much valuable time which could be concentrated on the main work of the Abbey. The cows were replaced by sheep which included a flock of Jacobs.

The vegetable gardens had been the only part of the estate which had been consistently maintained since the days when Lee Abbey was a private house. These had provided a useful supply of fruit and vegetables for the hotel and for the school. When rationing continued after the war it became essential for the Community to maintain the gardens, along with the two greenhouses. Rabbits caught on the estate were also frequently on the menu. Community members kept chickens, ducks and pigs. The vegetable garden took up 2½ acres, with a further acre of flower beds. The gardens supplied the bulk of vegetables used in the house, apart from potatoes.

An aerial view of the Abbey in 1955 showing the extensive vegetable gardens.

At work in the greenhouses.

Community members help prepare the vegetables in 1953.

In 1974 a new kitchen was constructed in the old inner courtyard, part of the original seventeenth-century farmhouse. As usual the work was undertaken by skilled local labour and Community members as labourers. This enabled the dining room to be extended and a canteen area to be constructed.

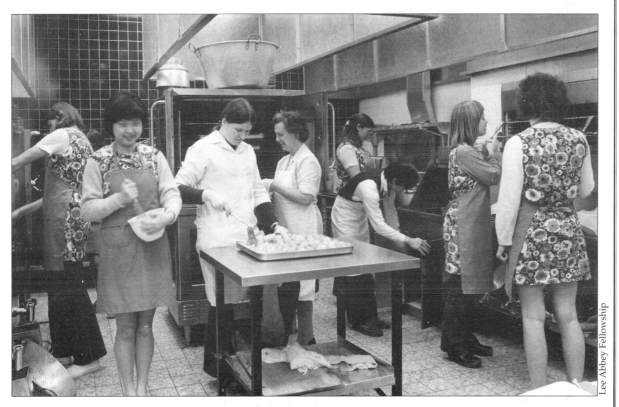

Community members at work in the new kitchen.

The Top Lodge was threatened by a large fire in the Valley of Rocks at Easter 1956. It was then lived in by the junior chaplain and his wife, who had to be evacuated with their furniture. Luckily the wind changed direction at the last moment.

The Top Lodge in 1955.

The gate next to the Top Lodge in 1955. The road past the Abbey is a public bridleway but a private highway. For many years the Top Lodge was the tollkeeper's cottage before transfer to the Bottom Lodge near the beach.

Lee Abbey Fellowship

Lee Abbey Fellowship

The tea garden at Lee Mouth Cottage was purchased by the Fellowship in 1961 from Mrs Budd, whose father had been woodsman for Squire Bailey. There she had maintained a well-known cream tea business, formerly known as Miss Delbridge's Tea Gardens. The first members of the Community to live in it were Lily Lloyd, a cook, and Ursula Kay, who ran the farm. They continued the cream teas but Lily died not long after. Part of the adjoining field was made into the garden as a memorial. Ursula joined the Community in 1955 and ran the tea garden after the death of Lily. She died whilst at Lee Mouth Cottage in 1984, having provided a vital sense of continuity in the early days of the Community. She had a great love of nature and her nature notes and sketches were later published as a book. Her collection of natural objects became a small museum alongside the path to the beach. Unfortunately, this disappeared with the erection of a new block of public toilets for the beach car park. At the same time the adjoining Pelton House, which once housed the Pelton Wheel for generating hydro-electric power, was converted as accommodation for retired members of the Community. The author well remembers sharing guided walks with Ursula and the great enthusiasm she imparted to the public for wildlife and the work of the Abbey.

Edna Madgwick

Ursula Kay.

Lee Abbey has had summer youth camps since 1947. The first was a small camp on Crock Point but from the next year they were regularly held in the field above the beach and below Lee Mouth Cottage. The camps became well established during the 1950s under the leadership of Raymond Scantlebury, followed by Ray Fardon. They have been run separately from the activities at the house.

From a local postcard.

The camp site in 1953.

In the 1950s campers were mostly aged between twenty and thirty but with the ending of National Service the average age reduced and teenagers became the main age group. The camps were organised for two fortnights in August, with the second fortnight later becoming two separate one-week camps. Activities at the camp are largely unstructured, with the main focus being on the evening epilogue.

Campers in 1956.

Numbers attending each camp ranged up to about 150. Since the 1980s, despite improvements in facilities, the camps have proved less attractive to more sophisticated youngsters. At the time of writing in 2003 a new indoor youth centre is being erected on the site of the former farm buildings.

The youth camp in the 1980s.